Chakras Healing Meditation for Beginners

How to Balance the Chakras and Radiate Positive Energy

Robin McGill

Table of Contents

Introduction

Congratulations on purchasing this book, and thank you for doing so. This book will help you in developing a clear understanding of the concept and importance of chakras, the reasons for their blockage and the ways to heal them.

The concept of chakras has started to attract the attention of people these days as most people feel that it can help them in addressing most of their problems in life.

The concept of chakras is very deep and wide. In the east, this concept was developed more than 4000 years ago, and since then it is being followed in various forms. If you look closely, the knowledge of chakras can help you solve a lot of mysteries of your personal life. The best thing about chakras is that it just doesn't tell about the problems but also helps you in finding the solutions.

There are several myths and misconceptions that float around the concept of chakras. There is a lack of clarity, and most people still consider it to be some form of magic. There are people who maintain a distance from the knowledge of chakras as they believe it pertains to a specific religion.

This book will help you in clearing all such confusions.

This book is just not an introduction to the concept of chakras but would also explain in detail the ways in which you can benefit from this knowledge.

We all have these chakras active in our bodies naturally. However, modern lifestyle, stress, anxiety, repressed emotions, chronic pain, and general suffering of life can block the chakras, and the smooth energy flow in the may get affected. It can cause innumerable problems, and after reading the book, you'll also be able to assess the number of problems that you have been facing due to chakra blockage. Our ignorance makes us continue on the same path without any respite.

Chakra blockage can be rectified, and chakras can be healed. This means most of the problems caused by the chakras don't need to be a permanent part of our lives. They can be removed permanently.

This book will help you in understanding the ways in which you can make that happen.

Most people believe that it might be a very difficult task and may need great expertise or skill. This book will explain the simple ways in which the chakra issues can be corrected.

I assure that you will find the solutions easy and effective.

I hope that you will find this book useful and would be able to add value through the knowledge in this book.

There are plenty of books on this subject on the market, thanks again for choosing this one! Every effort was made to ensure it is full of as much useful information as possible; please enjoy it!

Chapter 1: What are Chakras?

In the past few decades, the concept of 'Chakras' has gained fair recognition in the western world. It is viewed with great interest as a mystical concept that has the power to solve complicated issues.

- Some people look at 'Chakras' as a way to find inner peace. They seek the power of chakras to find a way out of the conundrum of life.

Are they on the right path?

Eastern cultures have been following this path for more than 4000 years now. The practice hasn't just remained confined to one region but kept on widening its spread, and this is proof that did get the intended benefits. Chakras can help you in finding peace and tranquillity.

- Some see 'Chakras' as a medium to restore the lost energy balance. Through the power of chakras, they try to find the lost spark in their lives.

Does the energy balance matter, or is it even a real thing?

The importance of energy balance may vary from person to person. However, it is no secret that without an inherent energy balance, it can become very difficult to carry out the functions of this life seamlessly.
Either it is the sheer lack of interest in life or inability to channelize the energies in positive ways, the chakras can help in the energy work.

- Others think that through the power of 'Chakras,' they will be able to express their inherent abilities better.

Are they misguided in thinking so?

People struggling in their lives and career do get an uncanny feeling that they are trapped in the wrong professions. Their passions and abilities lie somewhere else. Whatever amount of effort they put in a particular profession or art form, they are never able to achieve their true potential. Whereas, on the other hand, there are people who start getting fame and success effortlessly. They seem to be in the right place at the right time. This isn't just a matter of coincidence.

This book will explain the ways chakras influence our personality, characteristic traits, tastes, and professional abilities.

If you work on the correct chakras as per your interest and inclination, there is no limit to the abilities you can gain in those fields. We are a sum total of the way our energies get manifested. The energy is like an electrical current. You can use the same energy to heat water or freeze it. It all depends on the appliance being used. The chakras are those mediums. If you work on the correct chakras as per your inclination, you can reach your maximum potential easily.

This book will help you in understanding chakras and the way in which they matter for us. The concept of Chakras is not based on superstitious beliefs. Well established practices like 'Reiki Healing' are based on the energy flow principles of chakras. The science of acupuncture and acupressure also work on energy flow principles.

It is a concept that was followed in various forms in most parts of the world, even when there was no way to spread knowledge. This means that our ancestors felt the significance of energy flow in our lives. The Chakra concept has this principle well developed and organized. For thousands of years, the sages meditated on the concept and helped develop it to perfection.

In the chakra system, there are set principles that can help you in bringing perfect energy balance. With the help of chakra healing, you can restore open blocked chakras, activate the inactive chakras, and bring all the chakras in sync. In fact, there are several ways to bring this harmony.

All this has taken thousands of years of practice and work. It is an age-old tradition that has been perfected with time and patience.

By simply following some specific rules and practices, you can get all the benefits of the chakra system. The only thing that stands between you and the world of knowledge is your ignorance about this concept.

The main purpose of this book is to help you understand the concept from scratch so that you can explore it without doubts in your mind.

- You may have doubts in your mind.
- You may be a cynic.
- You may be a skeptic.

In fact, being all of this is good and encouraged in the eastern traditions.

The earliest documented mention of the chakra system is found in the Hindu tradition of the Indus valley foundation. The Hindu tradition, as we know it not a tradition of believers. It doesn't ask you to believe in established principles. It wants you to question things. It wants you to question established beliefs. It wants you to first understand every principle that you are going to work on.

It is a tradition that encourages the exploration of knowledge. Even the ancient religious Hindu texts are full of questions and answers. In this tradition, people have never hesitated to ask questions even from God. In fact, they have always sought answers to the most complex problems in life.

Therefore, if you want to proceed as a skeptic or a cynic, you are most welcome to do that.

Some people fear that the practice of chakra might interfere with their faith.

Such people have no reason to worry. Although the mention of chakras originated in the ancient Hindu texts, the practice was never developed as a religious practice. It is simply a way to channelize your energies in the right manner.

In fact, the practice of Yoga also originated in the same texts. But, the whole world today has acknowledged and accepted its benefits. It has nothing religious to it. It is a simple practice of keeping the body and the mind healthy.

In the same way, Chakra meditation also has nothing religious attached to it. Chakra practice is a simple way of channelizing your energies in the right direction.

- If you feel that your life is not going in the right direction
- If you feel lost midway
- If you feel energy drained
- If you feel confused and chaotic
- If you find incapable of utilizing your energies to their full potential

Then, the exploration of the concept of chakras is a must for you.

Chakras can help you in achieving these goals and much more. In fact, the powers of chakras are infinite.

However, simply pursuing the Chakras for the sake of these goals without understanding them a bit wouldn't be prudent.

This book is going to help you with three main things:

1. Explain the concept of chakras.
2. Make you aware of the power of chakras.
3. Help you heal and balance the chakras.

Chapter 2: History of the Concept of Chakras

Introduction of Chakras to the Western World

Just a few decades ago, the mention of chakras would have failed to ring any bell in the hearts and minds of people. Yet today, the concept of chakras is the talk of the town.

The concept of chakra is around 100 years old for the western world. In the year 1919, Sir John Woodroffe who was appointed as the Advocate General of Bengal by the then British imperial government during the period of India's colonization. Bengal is an eastern state in India. During his 18 years of stay in India, Sir Woodroffe developed a deep interest in the Sanskrit studies.

He studied Sanskrit during his stay in India and translated some 20 original Sanskrit texts. He was especially interested in the philosophy of the Chakra system, and to take that knowledge to the western world; he published his landmark work 'The Serpent Power' in 1919. This is the first book in English that talks about the concepts of Kundalini Yoga and Chakras in detail.

Historical Reference of Chakras

The earliest mention of Chakras is found to be more than 4000 years old. Excavated Sanskrit text detailing chakras are some of the oldest references available to us. However, it is believed that the concept of chakras may be as old as the practice of meditation, which can extend this timeline much farther as proofs of meditation practices are more than 8000 years old.

It is very hard to tell the exact timeline of the chakra meditation concept as Hindu Vedic traditions were mainly oral in nature. The teachers, sages, and seers passed on the knowledge to their deserving disciples through practical training and verbal medium. Many a time, the teachers even allowed several teachings to die if they were unable to find a deserving disciple as they feared misuse of knowledge or incorrect propagation. The tradition of preserving knowledge through books and written material came into practice very late.

Ancient Hindu texts called Vedas and Upanishads have elaborate descriptions of chakras. There are several Upanishads that have a detailed description of chakras and their uses in our personal lives.

Propagation of the Idea of Chakra Meditation

The idea of chakra meditation started to spread rapidly as Buddhism grew. The Buddhist monks who went around the world, spreading the word of peace through meditation, also carried the chakra concept as both were complimentary to each other. Meditation makes it very easy to bring a balance in the chakras, and if the chakras are in balance, finding peace in life becomes very easy. This is a blend that's effortless and desirable. The terminologies changed, some concepts were merged, but the whole concept was interwoven perfectly. Several healing techniques followed around the world are an example of this.

For instance, Reiki healing is a technique that was developed in Japan. It works on similar principles as Chakras. Acupuncture, acupressure, yoga, reflexology, and Qigong are some other techniques that seem to be based on the same lines.

Here, it is important to note that these techniques didn't originate at the same place. Some techniques developed in India, whereas others took birth in far-flung regions of Asia like China and Japan. This may not look tough today, but think of the speed with which things could spread 2000 years ago. These are indigenous techniques to those regions.

The concept of energy is universal in nature. Learned people all around the world felt this energy and tried to build a system that can help them channelize it in a better way. Think about the chakra system as one of the most well-defined and structured systems in this series.

Clearing Some Confusions

The concept of chakra is very wide. The power of chakras is unlimited, and there should be no doubt about that. However, there are several myths circulated about this concept.

Some people want to bank on the idea of chakras, and hence they started projecting it as a concept of gaining great mystical powers. Others have put it as some magical power in front of the masses. This creates a big layer of mysticism and apprehension.

The concept of chakras holds no bigger magic than the magic of you. We are full of great potential, and it is an indisputable fact. Chakras can definitely help in enhancing those inherent abilities inside you, and that may look like some magic work to others. However, this takes time, patience, and a lot of work. The people who are not paying attention think that the other person has become outstanding overnight.

The famous quote of Lionel Messi is very apt in this context. He said, " I start early, and I stay late, year after year, it took me 17 years and 114 days to become an overnight success.".

There are others who treat Chakras as some dark magic concept like Voodoo. Chakra is not a concept that affects others. It is a way to improve yourself. You can improve yourself through this technique. You can develop your powers. What you do with that power is always up to you, and the technique has nothing to do with that.

However, as you gain a better understanding of the concept of chakras, you will learn that as you move up the chakra ladder, your sense of self-obsession starts diminishing. You become less self-centered or concerned. You start feeling more connected and concerned with the world.

The concept of chakras has the end-goal of creating universal identify and merging the self into it. It helps you in widening the reaches of your perception and relate better to the needs of the whole world around you.

The Vedic culture has never been the one obsessed with the accumulation of material possessions, but of knowledge and the concept of chakras is a testimony of that.

In the past few years, people have started showing a keen interest in chakras, especially in the awakening of the sixth chakra, also known as the Third Eye Chakra or Ajna chakra. The reason for this keen interest lies in the fact that this chakra can help a person in gaining psychic powers. It also helps in extending the sense of perception and sixth sense.

The problem is that if you try to awaken the third eye chakra without working on other chakras in your body, it can create an energy imbalance. The very power that you wanted to use for your advantage can start scaring you as it can easily go out of control. Learning the art of properly managing and channelizing this energy is very important.

Chapter 3: Why do You Need to Know About Chakras?

This is one of the most valid questions that may arise in your mind. The chakras may be very powerful, but harnessing the power of chakras is not going to be a cakewalk. It would need time, patience, and perseverance.

Learning anything in life isn't easy. Learning to walk is such a simple act. It is a skill that is inside our cellular memory. Our body has limbs and muscles specifically designed to make us walk. Yet, a child needs months of practice to learn the art of walking. Similarly, our minds and bodies are fully capable of harnessing the power of chakras, but they would require practice and patience.

However, before you put in all that time and effort, it is very obvious to ponder over the basic question of utility.

Let us have a look at the following questions.

1st Chakra Problems:

Do you have a general feeling of lack of energy, vigor, and vitality?

Do you feel that you severely lack confidence outside your comfort zone?

Is there a general fearfulness inside you about family and security?

Do you mostly find yourself indecisive or find it hard to stick to a decision?

Are you finding it really difficult to get a promotion at work?

These are some of the signs of problems in the Root chakra.

2nd Chakra Problems:

Do you feel that you are losing passion even about things you loved the most?

Is there a general disinterest in enjoying the pleasures of life?

Do you feel that your sex life is getting boring or dull without an apparent reason?

Is your sense of self-worth becoming increasingly fragile?

Have you constantly started looking for appreciation?

Has guilt of the past mistakes started taking over you as a person?

These are some of the signs of problems in the Sacral chakra.

3rd Chakra Problems:

Are you struggling to maintain boundaries?

Do you feel a general sense of poor self-control?

Have you started feeling utterly demotivated?

Have you started feeling more drawn towards addictions?

Have you started leaning on others for your work lately?

These are some of the signs of problems in the Solar Plexus chakra.

4th Chakra Problems:

Are you losing your sense of identity or facing an internal identity crisis?

Have misunderstandings in relationships or with family members have started to rise exponentially?

Are you finding it really difficult to get a creative outlet?

Have you started saying yes to everyone and everything?

Are you experiencing trust issues?

Are you finding it really difficult to let go of the past and move on?

Do you feel emotions bottled up inside you?

These are some of the signs of problems in the Heart chakra.

5th Chakra Problems:

Have you started to find it really difficult to express yourself?

Is learning anything new becoming very difficult?

Do you feel that you are becoming increasingly stubborn?

Is there an increasing sense of detachment?

Are you becoming really intolerant of listening to others?

Have you started losing your grip or influence over others?

These are some of the signs of problems in the root chakra.

6th Chakra Problems:

Have you started feeling too much disconnected and confused?

Do you feel stuck to problems with an inability to look beyond?

Are you becoming over judgmental lately?

Do you feel gripped by stress and anxiety?

Are you losing the distinction between fiction and reality?

Are you finding it hard to believe in anything?

These are some of the signs of problems in the Third Eye chakra.

7th Chakra Problems:

Do you find yourself getting lofty and pompous?

Are your beliefs becoming rigid?

Have you started behaving secretive, obsessive, and hypocritical?

Do you feel general disorientation?

Have you started feeling uninspired?

Are you becoming overly sensitive to light?

These are some of the signs of problems in the Crown chakra.

Do you feel some of the questions hitting close to home?

These are some of the problems that can arise if there is an imbalance in the chakras. The actual list of problems that can arise due to chakra imbalance is very long. You will get to know about the problems in greater detail when we discuss the chakras individually.

Here, the purpose of this chapter is to simply explain to you the reasons you need to learn more about the chakras. Most of the time, the problem simply lies in the chakras, which can be addressed easily; however, we are generally trying to find it in something else, and that's why it never gets resolved. The chakra knowledge can help you in addressing many such issues easily.

The concept of chakras is not something that only concerns people who want to gain something out of the ordinary. It related to every person who wants peace in life and wants to succeed.

The knowledge chakras can be your map to move straight to your destination.

Does that mean you won't reach your destination if you don't have the map? Most likely, you know the answer already.

You may or may not reach the destination. However, you'll definitely find it comparatively difficult and time-taking to reach there.

In simple words, chakra knowledge can serve the purpose of a general guide in life. It is also a training manual with which you can work on the required areas in a much-focused way.

If you want to succeed in any specific field, you can start working on strengthing the chakra that helps in developing those abilities. For instance, when we begin studies, we need to study many subjects. We are at a tender age, and hence all the subjects are taught so that we can develop a better understanding to pick the stream of our liking. Now, imagine being forced to study all the subjects forever, or the subjects you have no interest in.

The knowledge of chakra can save you this inconvenience in life. You will know the things you like and need to work on. You will be able to detect problems better and faster. You will be more independent and content.

Knowledge is a great treasure, and the knowledge of chakras can become a treasure you'd never like to lose.

Chapter 4: The Science Behind Chakras

The ancient Vedic system describes the chakras as the energy centers. It believes that our existence is simply not in the form of this body. We exist on several other levels too. The Vedic system says that we exist at least on two other levels at the same time. Besides our physical body, there is also an energy body that exists around our physical body and then the spiritual body that surrounds everything else.

Scientists found it really hard to believe this fact, but it has been proven conclusively now that there is a field of aura around us. There is technology available that makes it possible to click pictures of this aura even after we have left that place. The energy field is so strong that it leaves its imprint even after you have left that place. It gets even more interesting from here.

The aura not only represents your physical presence but also gives a correct description of your mental and emotional state. This means that if you are feeling gloomy and discouraged, it will get reflected in the aura photography irrespective of the façade you present in the form of a phony smile. Your energy body is way more exact in representing your mental and emotional state.

Energy plays a very important role in our lives. While modern science and technology kept its focus entirely on physicality and matter, for centuries, the eastern sages and seers were busy looking inwards. They believed that there was more than just blood and bones to the human body. The sages believed that even if they designed something which could be made to work exactly in the same manner as human body functions, it wouldn't gain human characteristics and powers. Besides the mechanical function of the human body, there is energy that runs this body, and it is indestructible.

The Vedas proclaimed thousands of years ago that the soul is indestructible and incorruptible. This body is simply a carrier. The soul changes the body as one changes old clothes.

They called this energy 'Prana.' Prana in Sanskrit means life or universal life energy. This prana dictates all the mechanical as well as the emotional functions of the body.

The Vedas describe this energy system to be very elaborate in nature. They say that this energy flows alongside the nervous system in the body. There are 72000 main 'Nadis' or nerves that carry the 'Prana' throughout the body. The energy distribution network is so elaborate that for better control, it is divided into 114 sub-stations called chakras.

Therefore, the actual number of chakras in our body is 114 in total. 2 Chakras out of these, 114 are out of the body. This means they aren't physically present inside our body. We don't need to do anything in specific to keep those 2 chakras in balance. As long as all the other chakras are in balance, those 2 chakras will work in tandem.

The remaining 112 chakras are further divided into 7 groups. These groups control various aspects of our physical, emotional, and spiritual development. Under every major chakra, there are 16 minor chakras.

There is a popular misconception that the chakras are physically located inside the body. This is incorrect. In fact, there is nothing physical about chakras.

The word 'Chakra' in the Sanskrit language means a wheel. Now, as we have already discussed, the Parana flows through our nervous centers. The major meeting points of the nadis through which the Prana follows are known as chakras. But, the meeting points aren't circular. On the contrary, the nerves usually meet crisscrossing each other. The junction points are, therefore, always triangular. However, energy as we know it is flowing, it is in a fluid form. Hence, at the junction points, when energies from various sources meet, they create a spinning vortex of energy. It acquires a circular form, and it is moving, and that's why it is called chakra.

Everything in the body is closely connected. The 112 chakras or the junction points form a direct link with each other. They remain in a network. However, there is nothing like a wheel working inside you. You won't find freewheels inside you like there are in a watch. The point where the confluence of energy is very powerful is called a chakra. In this way, there are 112 such points in the body. However, there needs to be a system to regulate this flow of energy in an appropriate manner. The power centers of energy that can regulate the flow of energy inside our body. Those power centers are the main 7 chakras, and they are located outside the body.

The location of the chakras is alongside the spine. There are seven major points that are said to be the locations of the chakras. The locations are not based on assumptions. Each major chakra influences an endocrine gland as well as a group of nerves called plexus. The endocrine glands are ductless glands that have the power to influence most of the functions in the body through the production of chemical messengers known as hormones. The plexus can transmit messages directly to the affected regions. Therefore, the chakras can dominate every aspect of your being without even being physically located inside the body.

Each chakra has a strong association with an endocrine gland and a plexus or a group of nerves. This gives them the complete control mechanism of the body. The 7 chakras can strongly influence your physical, emotional, mental, and spiritual health at the same time.

Many people who know a little bit about chakras and have got fascinated by the powers of one specific chakra make a fatal mistake of considering these chakras separate entities. Although each chakra has its influence on a specific endocrine gland and nerve center, it is closely connected to the other chakras. Simply working on one chakra is only going to complicate the chakras, as this will disturb the delicate energy balance.

For instance, the lower three chakras in the body connect you strongly to your body. They keep you focused on material pursuits and self-preservation. The upper three chakras are strongly connected to intellectualism and spirituality. They are always trying to break you free from the desire for self-gratification and self-preservation. Yet, even if you want to gain spiritual knowledge, your root chakra must be open, active, and balanced. Without a working root chakra, you can't have a functional crown chakra as the first chakra is the ladder to the second chakra and upwards. You can neither jump the chakras nor bypass them.

The energy through the central nervous system will only flow and transmit smoothly when all the chakras are working in harmony.

Irrespective of the kind of powers you want or the chakra you want to focus on, it is very important that all the chakras in your body remain active, open, and balanced.

Chapter 5: The Importance of Chakra Balancing

As we have already discussed, there are 7 major chakras. The role of chakras is to regulate energy at each level and pass it on to the next chakra in the line. The chakras in the body are not the source of this energy. They are simply transforming this energy and then passing it on to the upper chakras. To maintain physical, mental/emotional, and spiritual health, it is important that there is a smooth and unobstructed flow of energy. If any chakra is blocked or inactive, the flow of energy will get affected. Every chakra has its own area of importance. It influences a set of characteristics and no other chakra can have anything to do with it. Blockage in one any chakra is going to affect you.

However, this doesn't mean that every chakra is the same. The level of intensity with which you experience life at a chakra keeps increasing as you move up the chakra ladder. You start experiencing life more vigorously. For instance, if there is an energy imbalance in the lower chakras like the root chakra, the impact would be visible only in limited areas. You will personally get more affected, but the people around you may not be able to experience the difference as the changes might be very subtle. However, if there is an energy imbalance in the upper chakras like the third eye chakra or crown chakra, the signs would be visible more clearly. The reason is very simple: the intensity with which you experience life at these levels is very high. This is a reason that people give more importance to the upper chakras. However, that's a mistake that you must not make.

Every chakra caters to specific qualities and gives you a push in that direction. It has a specific role that can't be ignored. For instance, many people who have recently developed knowledge about chakras feel fascinated by the third eye chakra. It is a chakra that, upon being fully active, can give you a heightened sense of perception. This chakra can give you strong psychic powers. It can make your sixth sense very powerful, and you may be able to sense energies around you. All this sounds great and exciting. However, people generally ignore the power required to hold this kind of power.

There is no doubt that the third eye chakra will increase your psychic abilities. But, it works both ways. You'll get the power to sense energies around you, but that doesn't mean you'll really be prepared to deal with them 24X7. You cannot have any control over what kind of energies come in contact with you. When this starts happening in an uncontrolled manner, it can frighten you. Your ability to perceive things increases several folds. However, this also doesn't mean that you'll be thinking only about the positive things. Your thoughts may be guided by the things around you, and they are of mixed nature. It also means that you can start having really negative thoughts. If you are not properly grounded, you may start feeling really frightened. You may lose grip over your thoughts. To remain grounded in reality, you need to have a strong and active root chakra. Without a powerful root chakra, you'll stand like a weak pole with a heavy load in a heavy storm. One stong blow will have the capability to topple you over, and even the smaller ones will keep shaking you forever.

Therefore, as you need the upper chakras for greater powers, you also need lower chakras to develop the ability to hold those powers. Apart from that, the way to open the upper chakras properly also goes through the lower chakras.

Balanced chakras help in the smooth functioning of the mind and the body. They help in the overall development of your personality. The chakras also give shape to your personality. The strongest chakra in your system will give you a defining shape. This means that if the upper chakras in your body are more prominent, then you will have a stronger personality. This is also a reason why people are so persuasively after the upper chakras. However, here also the same rule applies. Without the development of the lower chakras, the expression of the upper chakras would never be helpful. If you try to get this in an unnatural way or with excessive effort, then the chances of things getting wrong are very high.

I want to really stress this point time and again as people make this mistake very often. They are only after specific chakras without actually understanding the mechanics of energy. You can only get the benefits of active chakras when all your chakras are in sync. Even one blocked chakras can put your body and mind out of balance.

Another thing which is really important to understand that it is not only the blockage of the chakra that can cause a problem. Even if a chakra becomes overactive, it can cause the same amount of problems or even more. Chakras are powerful energy centers, if they become overactive, the same qualities that can help you will start causing problems.

For instance, the second chakra called the Sacral Chakra enables you to enjoy the fruits of this world. It gives you the ability to feel joy and pleasure in this world. It also gives you the desire to have sexual pleasures. This chakra binds you strongly to this world.

If the energy flow to this chakra is low, you may start feeling disinterested in everything. You may neither seek pleasure nor find it anywhere. This can strain relationships and may also make you bitter and resentful. This is the chakra that makes you love this world and life. Without it in your life, this world would become dull.

However, if the energies in this chakra become overactive, it can make you obsessed. You can become a person completely drawn to pleasures. You'd also become completely indifferent to all your responsibilities and the people around you. Overexpression of energy in the Sacral chakra can also make you a sex maniac who has nothing else on the mind besides sex. Such people start looking at everyone and everything as sex objects. These people don't remain hidden for long in societies and get branded or outclassed very soon. These people also lose their utility for society soon and end-up living a resentful life.

This was just an example of an energy imbalance in one chakra. The sacral chakra is still a lower chakra, and hence its intensity is low. As you move up, the intensity would increase, and hence, the impact felt on your life and personality would be much greater.

Therefore, it is very important that you work towards harmonizing your chakras. The more they work in sync, the better your life would become.

Chapter 6: The 7 Chakras and Their Properties

There are 7 main chakras:

Number	**Name of the Chakra**	**Sanskrit Name**	**Associated Gland**
1st Chakra	The Root Chakra	Mooladhara	Adrenal Cortex Gland
2nd Chakra	The Sacral Chakra	Svadisthana	Ovaries and testicles
3rd Chakra	The Solar Plexus Chakra	Manipura	Pancreas
4th Chakra	The Heart Chakra	Anahata	Thymus
5th Chakra	The Throat Chakra	Vishuddhi	Thyroid
6th Chakra	The Third Eye Chakra	Ajna	Pituitary
7th Chakra	The Crown Chakra	Sahasrara	Pineal

The chakras are very powerful, and they just don't affect us physically but also on several other levels too. Broadly, the impact of chakra can be felt on four different levels:

1. Physically
2. Mentally
3. Emotionally
4. Spiritually

Every chakra has its characteristic properties. If that chakra is functioning normally, you will have certain functionalities that would be working fine. Any kind of imbalance that involves lower energy in that chakra or overactive chakra may completely change the way that chakra functions.

In this chapter, we will try to understand in detail the levels on which each chakra affects our lives and the impact energy imbalance in any chakra can have on our lives.

Before we begin, it is important to understand that the list of characteristics mentioned here is not exhaustive. In fact, no book can be as exhaustive to cover the full extent of the chakras. Here, we will try to develop an understanding of the power chakras wield on our lives, although they remain completely hidden out of the picture.

Out of the 7 chakras, the lower three chakras are directly concerned with the body. Their main objective is to try to keep you strongly attached to this world. Feelings of self-assertion, self-gratification, and self-definition are very important at the level of these chakras. In a way, they are working towards self-preservation.

The upper three chakras work in a completely different direction. Their aim is to provide knowledge and take you towards liberation. Their main objective is self-reflection and self-knowledge. Like the two poles in a magnet, the upper and lower chakra work on different goals. One is trying to make you work towards self-preservation while the other is seeking liberation from this world.

The fourth chakra is the bridge. It is in the center, and hence it has the tendency of both types. It has an affinity towards love but also an attraction towards creativity, which ultimately leads to liberation.

You should never classify any chakra as good or bad and powerful or weak. Every chakra has its place in the 7 chakra system. The impact which may look small here will be much different from personal experience.

The Root Chakra- Mooladhara

This chakra is represented by a bright red color. This chakra is dense. It is basic in nature. The prime feeling on this level is self-preservation. This chakra has the gravitation element. It keeps you tied to your roots and helps you in remaining grounded in reality. Order, structure, and the need for logic are the basic things that this chakra strives to achieve. This chakra keeps you focused on the five senses.

The Sanskrit meaning of the word 'Moola' is root or basic. This is the basic chakra. It becomes active even before you come into this world. From your conception to around 12 months of age, this chakra is the dominant one in the body. The primary goals of this chakra are to achieve stability, physical health, and stability. Trust is a very important factor for this chakra, as it also relates to safety and security. This chakra longs for prosperity.

Balanced Root Chakra: This chakra is all about physicality, and hence a balanced root chakra would provide you unlimited physical energy. A person with a fully-functioning root chakra will have no problems in physically intense work. Sports and manual work would be of great enjoyment. Such a person would also be very centered and grounded. These are very important qualities and also the prime requisites of peace and happiness. This chakra doesn't long for much; it tries to find sufficiency in whatever is available. It can give you complete control over your desires, aspirations, and wants. Even a little can mean a lot for a person with a balanced root chakra, and this means that such a person would know the rare art of living a happy and content life. Such a person would feel highly secure and would remain connected to roots like the family.

Weak Root Chakra: If someone has a weak root chakra, it can leave that person physically weak. Such people face problems in remaining grounded and hence remain fearful. They lack confidence due to low physical energy and mostly find themselves unable to achieve goals. This is the chakra that ensures survival, but when the energy at this level is low, the chances of a person becoming self-destructive are very high. Relationships with the roots and family bonds are also weak for such people, and hence they can easily start feeling unloved or abandoned.

Overactive Root Chakra: Excessive energy in the root chakra also poses an equal amount of problems. Contentment is an important quality of this chakra, but when there is excess energy, it tends to make people greedy. Your addiction to wealth may have no limits. You may also want to hoard unlimited power and become dominating and egoistic. The sexual energy going out of hand is also a problem for such people.

Health Issues Related to Root Chakra: The physical location of this chakra is perineum, and it can lead to chronic lower back pain, constipation, urinary tract infection, immunity issues, kidney stones, irrational fears, depression, and financial problems.

At the core of this chakra, the main objective is survival. While you are in the womb of your mother, this chakra becomes active and remains the only and most active chakra in your body. The prime focus of this chakra is to ensure your survival. This is the chakra that puts the feeling of fear in your heart. In the initial stages, when a child knows and understands nothing, the child is still alert about dangers. If you haven't paid attention to this aspect, watch a toddler trying to stand, walk, or do any other act. This chakra has a very strong impact on your physicality and basic character attributes.

The Sacral Chakra

This second chakra is represented by a bright orange color. This is one of the most interesting chakras. This chakra opens up at around 6 months of age and becomes fully functional around the age of 2 years. This is one of the most interesting chakras. This chakra helps you develop a deeper bond with this world through all your five senses. This is the chakra of joy and happiness.

This chakra opens you to the wonders this world has to offer. It makes you more receptive. The Sanskrit meaning of the word 'Sva' means 'One's own.' This chakra makes you feel this world as your own. The word 'Svad' means 'to taste.' It helps you taste this world and all the bounties it holds through all the five senses. Till this chakra is in full bloom in your body, the external force would have to be applied to make you sad. You would remain happy and blissful naturally, just like the kids. They simply remain blissfully unaware of all the pain and suffering around them, completely immersed in the games invented by them. They don't need anything specific to remain fully engaged. They'd simply find anything around themselves that's completely immersive. This is the chakra of experiencing this world. The glands influenced by this chakra are the reproductive glands. That's why this chakra is also responsible for arousing sexual feelings when the time comes.

Balanced Sacral Chakra: If the energy in this chakra is balanced and it is active, it will impart a sense of belonging. This chakra makes you very friendly and highly optimistic. This chakra helps you receive joy from all the things in the world, and your imagination would get fertile ground. This also gives a great push to your creative talent. It also makes you very intuitive. You will have concern for other people around you and would also have a healthy sense of humor. You will remain sensitive to the feelings of others, and that also makes you a very likable person.

Weak Sacral Chakra: If your sacral chakra is blocked or it has low energy, you can appear to be an extremely shy and timid person. You would have no sense of belonging, and you may also be filled with fear, and you would hesitate from exploring anything new. Such people generally become overly sensitive and resentful. People with weak sacral chakra are generally self-negating and have lots of buried emotions. They find it very difficult to trust others and may have a very touchy temperament. Not only this, they have repressed sexual feelings. This is a reason such people can start feeling guilty about sex. Low energy in this chakra can also make them frigid or infertile. They may also face difficulties in conceiving.

Overactive Sacral Chakra: Having an overactive sacral chakra can also be an equally bigger problem. This chakra is all about enjoying the pleasures of this world and living for the pleasures of the self. However, if the energies in this chakra are charged up more than required, this chakra can make you emotionally explosive, aggressive, and overly ambitious. People tend to become very manipulative for fulfilling their desire to enjoy themselves.

This chakra gives wings to your imagination, but this is only good to an extent. If the energies in this chakra get out of hand, they can also make you overimaginative. You may not have any control over your thought and may start living in your own world of illusions. It can also easily make you overindulgent and self-serving as the main objective of this chakra is to enable you to enjoy the pleasures of this world.

The bigger problems start to arise when excess energy in this chakra starts affecting your sexual desires. You can start having obsessive thoughts about sex, and at one point, only sex may become your prime concern. Such people start considering everyone as a mere object of sexual satisfaction.

Health Issues Related to Sacral Chakra: Sexual potency issues and urinary tract infections are the main health issues that may come to haunt a person with an imbalance in this chakra. However, due to its physical location in the lower back region, it may also cause chronic lower back pain and gynecological problems.

The objective of this chakra is to connect you to this world. It helps you get immersed completely and start enjoying this world and develop a sense of belonging. This is the chakra of pleasure and joy. However, very soon, the pleasures can turn into obsessions if the energies go out of hand. In case, the energies are weak; you would become completely incapable of enjoying this world. Most people who, at some point in time, lose all interest in their passions, and the things they liked in the past suffer from this problem. The people who start developing obsessive tendencies and change completely in their behavior may be suffering from overactive energies in this chakra. This chakra is important as it keeps you connected and interested. It makes like pleasurable, but an imbalance in this chakra can be destructive for personality.

The Solar Plexus Chakra

This is the third chakra and one of the most important one that has a very strong impact on your personality and appearance to the outside world. As we have already discussed, as we move up the chakras, the experiential intensity would keep increasing. Out of the three chakras that affect your physicality, this chakra is at the top and hence, the most intense. It is represented by the bright yellow color of the rays of the sun. Like the rays of the Sun, it can illuminate your life.

In Sanskrit, this chakra is called Manipura. The word 'Mani' means jewels. The word 'Manipura' means 'the city of jewels.' This chakra actually works like the city of jewels in a person's life. It empowers you to achieve all that you want in your life. This is the chakra of action. This chakra gives you an insatiable appetite. If this chakra is working in sync, you can achieve anything you desire.

This chakra starts to open up at the age of two years and can become fully functional by the age of 4. However, it starts blossoming fully in the teens. This is the time you get really focused on your studies and career. This is the chakra of abilities and passions. It fills you with spontaneity. You don't take too long to ponder over thoughts and start believing in actions. Vitality is another character trait of this chakra. This chakra fills you with the strength of will, purpose, and determination. Self-esteem is another thing that starts becoming very important to you once this chakra starts becoming active. This is the chakra of self-definition. Ego-identity starts becoming very important for you and becomes a part of your personality.

Balanced Solar Plexus Chakra: Balanced energies in the solar plexus chakra make you a self-respective person. This doesn't make you haughty or arrogant. The sense of self-respect also makes you respect others. However, you will have a strong sense of personal power. You aren't afraid of life in general, and this sense of fearlessness makes you outgoing and cheerful.

The most distinguishing thing about this chakra is that it makes you act. It keeps propelling you towards your goals. You are able to find your gift and find the motivation to keep enhancing it. It makes you skillful and intelligent. You get the appetite to digest life. You don't feel dull or demotivated on your quest. It keeps the fire burning strongly in your belly.

The solar plexus chakra keeps you constantly in motion, but it also makes you feel completely relaxed. You always feel at home in whatever you are doing. New challenges are never a burden when the solar plexus chakra is balanced. You would enjoy any kind of physical activity, and it would fill you with more energy.

Weak Solar Plexus Chakra: An energy deficient solar plexus chakra is bad news. It hits your confidence the hardest. You lose your focus on action and start worrying more about the things others would think about you. This is a clear indicator that your solar plexus chakra is getting energy deficient. An unexplained confusion and loss of control over life is another indicator of the problems in the solar plexus chakra. People affected with low energy in this chakra also start feeling depressed as things don't seem to go their way. They require constant reassurances from others as they clearly lack confidence and self-determination. They may also start to exhibit tendencies of jealousy and distrust against others. Loss of appetite and poor digestion are physical signs of a problem in this chakra.

Overactive Solar Plexus Chakra: If this chakra becomes overactive, it can fill you with a false sense of superiority complex. You may become highly judgmental and start treating others poorly. Some people also start behaving as perfectionists demeaning others. Their sole objective is to portray themselves as the best. Excessive energy in this chakra would constantly make you look for chances to prove your excellence. It can make you a workaholic, and you may also lose respect for personal boundaries. This can also lead to a poor work-life balance. You may become highly demanding and also try to position yourself as overly intellectual. Such people start disrespecting any kind of authority and become resentful of it. They are simply trying to establish themselves as above everything, even the system. They tend to develop a liking to addictions to relax and may not find peace within themselves.

Health Issues Related to Solar Plexus Chakra: This chakra influences the pancreas, and hence all the systems related to it can get affected. Diabetes, pancreatitis, liver dysfunction, hepatitis, adrenal dysfunction, loss of appetite, anorexia, bulimia, and gastric ulcers are common problems faced by people with problems in this chakra.

This is a very important chakra as it helps you in establishing your authority in this world. This is a world of doers. Only the people who have been able to achieve something remarkable are remembered, and this chakra constantly strives to take you towards this goal. However, this is a high energy chakra, and hence, keeping it balanced is very important. Low or excessive energy in this chakra can influence your whole personality. The intensity of this chakra is such that the influence is clearly visible. Not only your inner personality but also your outward behavior also gets affected by this chakra. Therefore, it is important that you pay attention to the signs of imbalance in this chakra. There are many ways to keep this chakra balanced. One must always remember that this chakra is powerful, but this is just a means and not your ultimate goal. If you remain focused solely on this chakra, it can easily become overactive.

The Heart Chakra

This is the fourth chakra of the system and a unique one. The most peculiar quality of this chakra is that it holds the best of both worlds. This chakra lies in the center of the powers that want to keep you tied to this material world and the ones which are in constant pursuit of knowledge and liberation. This chakra gives you both. It not only helps you remain connected to the physical world but also trains you to get connected to the divine. A blend of heart and mind is what you get at this chakra.

This chakra is called 'Anahata' in Sanskrit. It means an unstruck sound. The powers of this chakra have no beginning or end. They are reverberations of the divine. This chakra brings the spark of creativity in you. If this chakra is active and functioning in your body, you will have a creative spark inside you. Irrespective of the profession you follow, the hobbies you have, or the talent you possess, you will have a keen sense of appreciation of some form of art. This creative spark is the middle ground. It engages your senses but also titillates your intellectual powers.

The heart chakra enables you to live life very intensely. You will have the ability to absorb things differently. You will know no bounds. This chakra is represented by a green color. It is the color of new life, beginnings, and compassion. Love and emotions will have a very big role in your life. You will feel a strong connection to the divine, and gratitude will have a special place in your life. You wouldn't be a person who simply ignores people. Giving and receiving would have equal importance in your life.

Balanced Heart Chakra: To be fair, this chakra is all about the delicate balance in life. It keeps you physically, emotionally, and spiritually balanced. The balanced heart chakra is very important for living a fulfilling life in this world. Without a balance in this chakra, you would always keep longing for one thing or the other, and contentment would always keep evading you.

Compassion, empathy, and gratitude are defining qualities of this chakra. This chakra has a unique nurturing quality about it. A person with a fully active and blossoming heart chakra will have the ability to heal the hidden wounds of people around him/her. That person would simply be a big magnet, and people would feel completely drawn towards him/her. This all happens because of the simple ability of understanding and empathy.

There is no reason to think that such people would be anything but friendly. They also have a strong desire to work for the community and would actively participate in social causes. Their humanitarian side would be visible from far. They would have an uncanny eye to see the good in others.

This chakra also gives people a great power of discernment. Such people would be able to easily dissect the facts and pick whatever is necessary. This is an intense chakra, and hence it also brings a strong will power and desire to help others.

Love and relationships will hold a very special place for people with the balanced heart chakra. They'd constantly be in love. It's not important for them to love an individual, their love can be for a cause, whole humanity, and even spirituality and god, but it would surely be there. Without love, this chakra can't function. Love is the fuel of this chakra.

Weak Heart Chakra: The first thing that strikes when this chakra gets deficient in energy is unworthiness in love. People start feeling lost and completely out of place. They may start needing constant reassurance as an integral part of the personality goes missing. Fear may overtake every major aspect of their personality. Fear of getting hurt is a primary fear as they are unable to form strong relationships. They also find it very hard to come out of the shadows of their past relationships due to the fear of letting go. They also experience a strange fear of being free. They have a fear of getting abandoned. All these fears make them paranoid.

They largely remain indecisive and impractical. They keep searching for shoulders to brood. The simple inability to form stable relationships and hold them together makes them miserable.

Overactive Heart Chakra: If the energies in the heart chakra become overactive, a person can become very moody and melodramatic. Such people love others conditionally and have a strange martyr complex. They can become highly demanding and possessive too. Trust remains a big problem here too, and hence they find it difficult to trust others. They develop a habit of withholding love and generosity. Their personality becomes maniac-depressive and such people become difficult to bear.

However, internally, such people are more difficult on themselves than others. They are overly critical about everything as their power of discernment is weak, and they fail to see the good in others. High blood pressure and cardiovascular diseases are big risks for such people.

Health Issues Related to Heart Chakra: Clearly, high blood pressure and heart problems remain high-risk issues. Such people may also remain prone to allergies and weak immune system. Breathing issues, pain in the upper back, and shoulders are also common in such people.

This is a chakra with a very delicate balance. This chakra is continuously striving to maintain balance. It lies between two polar opposites and serves as an axis. However, this is a chakra with a strong spiritual side. If this chakra blossoms in a person, the chances of attaining spiritual consciousness without actually having to open the upper chakra is also very high here. This chakra can help in the overall development of your outward and inward personality as a human being. The solar plexus chakra helps you come out as a strong and determined individual, but this chakra helps you mature into a stronger human being. The distinction is very big. You may find innumerable examples of strong individuals who have been able to achieve a lot in their lifetimes, but the number of people among them who were able to mature as matured human beings is very limited. This chakra doesn't become strong by possessing material wealth but with the help of spiritual consciousness.

From here, the upper three chakras have a different class of their own. Till here, the chakras mainly affected your personality as an individual, and they were more self-centered. Self-preservation and development were at the base of these chakras. However, the upper three chakras have completely different goals. Although these chakras also empower you and help you mature, they hone you to come out as a stronger human being.

These chakras make you more and more influential, and the powers that come with these chakras help you evolve as a person. These chakras constantly try to raise your level of consciousness. The powers that come with these chakras are boundless. The development of these chakras may make you a different person. Very seldom it happens that these chakras become powerful in a person, but that person still remains centered towards the self. They increase your power of expression, intellectuality, and consciousness. These three things may sound simple and vague here, but you'll see that when properly used, they can empower a person to become a true master of everything wished for.

The Throat Chakra

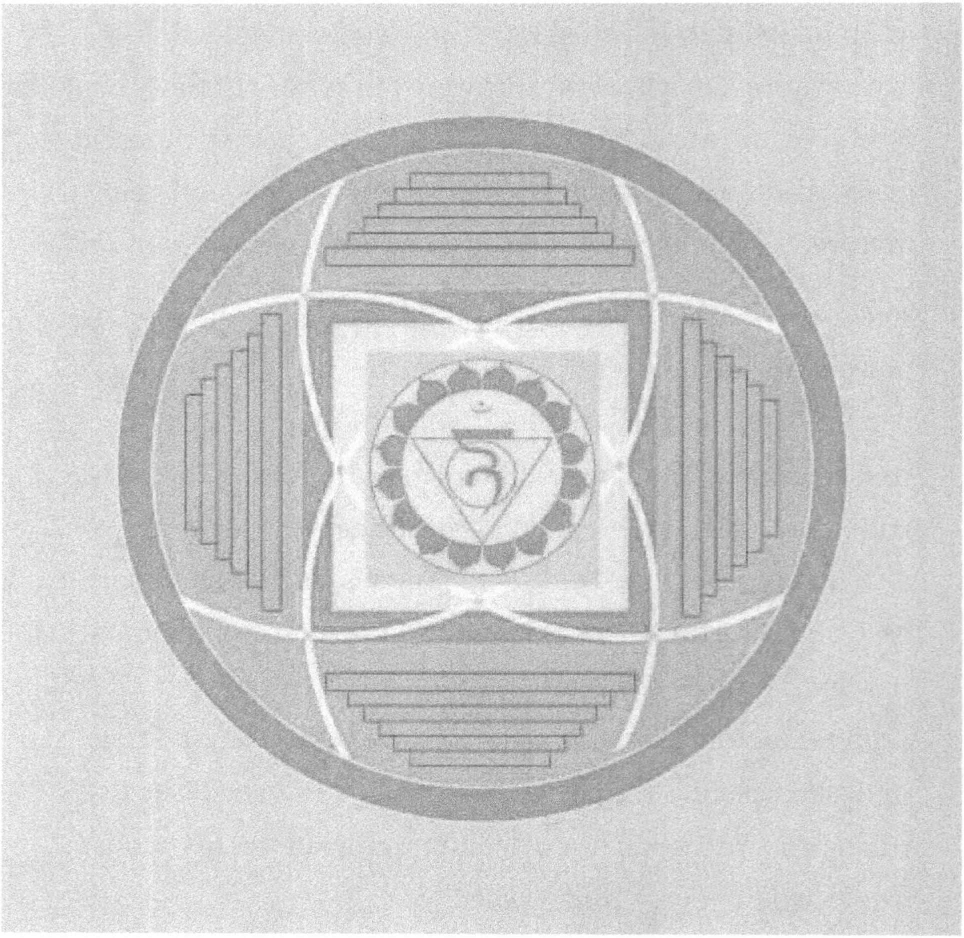

This fifth chakra of the system lies at the lower rung of the upper chakras. However, it is one of the most powerful chakras when it comes to gaining physical, intellectual, and influential powers and abilities. This is the center of gaining abilities, and people with a desire to gain occult powers specifically want to gain success over this chakra.

In Sanskrit, the word 'Vishuddhi' is made up of two words, 'Visha,' meaning poison, and 'Shuddhi' means to purify. At this level, all the impurities brought from the lower chakras get purified or filtered before you move to the chakras of the higher powers. The physical location of this chakra is in the throat, as the name clearly suggests. This chakra is a direct representation of a Hindu deity 'Shiva' or 'Rudra.' In fact, the whole chakra system is proposed to have been devised by Shiva in his mortal form. As per the stories in the Vedas, Shiva once drank all the poison of the world to clear this world of impurities so that life could survive. He didn't allow the poison to go down his throat, and as a result, his throat became blue. Interestingly, this chakra is also represented by a blue color. It is also the color body gets upon getting poisoned.

Hinduism represents it in the form of a dark blue color that the throat of Lord Shiva acquired after drinking the poison. Lord Shiva is also represented by garlanding a venomous snake around the neck, denoting the effect of poison in that region.

(Image of Hindu Deity Shiva garlanding a snake around his neck. The blue color at the neck also represents the effect of drinking and storing poison at that point.)

The Vedas state the throat as the point of 'Udan Prana' or the point from where your journey into higher consciousness begins. It is the point from where you travel into a deep sleep from waking sleep.

At the throat chakra, your consciousness starts to expand really fast. This is the chakra where you learn the art of handling an excessive amount of information and also the mastery in expressing it.

This is considered to be one of the most powerful chakras as it can increase your sphere of influence incredibly. If the energy blossoms in your throat chakra, you would have sway over everyone you want to communicate with. The recorded history of whole humankind is proof that not the men with swords or weapons but the men of words have ruled this world to date. With force, you can control some people for some time, but with words and ideas, you can make the whole world do your bidding.

A powerful throat chakra also makes learning new things very easy. You can easily gain mastery over things you've had no prior experience. This means if you want to gain access to your upper two chakras, it is very important to have a powerful throat chakra.

Balanced Throat Chakra: The biggest power that comes with a balanced throat chakra is the power to communicate effectively. You don't necessarily need words to communicate your message. There are several ways to communicate a message. This chakra simple opens the portal of communication for you.

This chakra brings you out of various time zones and establishes you in the present. This is a chakra of reality, purity, and clarity. It keeps you centered in the present. Your sense of timing and awareness of the present improve considerably. It makes you a terrific communicator. You'd find it effortlessly easy to communicate your message to others. Your thoughts and ideas wouldn't remain vague or hidden.

People with developed throat chakra are great communicators and artistically inspired. They would be expressive and prolific in whatever they do in personal and public life. This is the chakra of world leaders.

However, powers in this chakra would also mean that you'd be less concerned about your own self and more about others. Contentment is a thing that comes naturally with this chakra. When this chakra blossoms in someone, personal gains start looking like insignificant goals. A clear understanding of spiritual concepts develops in individuals with a powerful throat chakra. Such people are easily able to easily experience divine powers. They became capable of handling higher energies. They will also be able to handle and utilize their sexual energy in a better way. Balancing this chakra is very important before you start working on your third eye chakra, or the powers can easily go out of hand.

Weak Throat Chakra: Low energy in this chakra would be clearly visible in the form of poor communication abilities. The person would appear as a timid and overly quiet person who doesn't have the ability to express him/her well. Such people may also be highly inconsistent and unreliable. They may have a very poor sense of timing and may prefer to live in the past or in dreams. They may constantly find themselves at the crossroads of sex and religion. They would not be able to channelize their sexual energy properly. Nervousness and a devious nature is also a clear indicator of such people.

Overactive Throat Chakra: The energy at this level naturally gets very intense, and hence if it becomes overactive, the person may appear to be very dominating sexually and otherwise. It can get difficult to find the right outlet for this energy. Such people easily become self-righteous, and it becomes very difficult to convince them for anything. They may become very dogmatic, and there may not be many ways to change that to pragmatism until the energy balance gets restored. They can become overly talkative as communication comes as a natural gift. However, such people become prone to addictive tendencies as there are few things that can satisfy their physical and intellectual appetites.

Health Issues Related to Throat Chakra: As this chakra is directly connected to the throat and influences the thyroid gland, it can lead to thyroid issues and throat problems. Mouth ulcers, gum problems, laryngitis, and chronic soar throat are also some common issues.

The throat chakra is an important checkpoint for all those people who want to work on their upper chakras. It is highly advisable for those people to sincerely work on their throat chakra. This chakra can not only improve your understanding of the energies you are going to deal with but also prepares you for bearing them.

It is a power center of learning and developing abilities. With a powerful throat chakra, learning new things can become incredibly easy for any person. Knowledge would come swiftly and effortlessly. The gift of clear communication is another boon that comes with this chakra. If you are into public speaking or in some profession where you need to interact with others, working on this chakra is a must for you.

The Third Eye Chakra

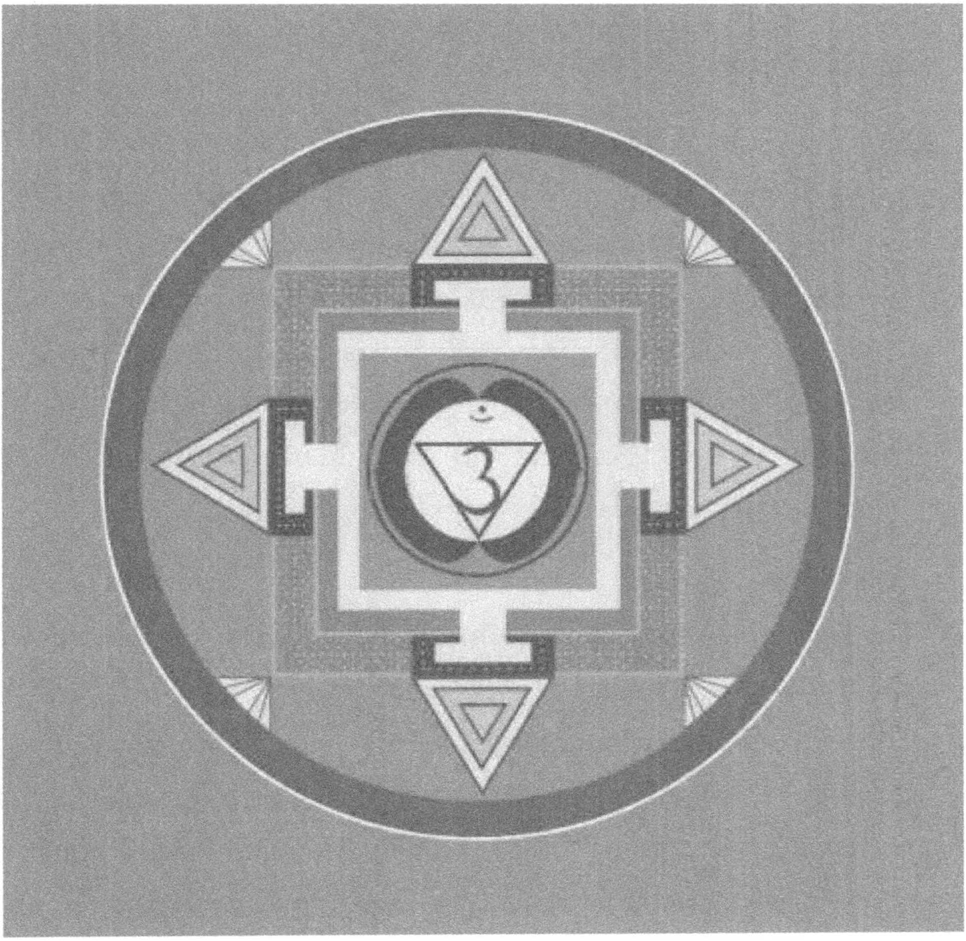

This is the sixth chakra and indisputably the most sought after chakra in the 7 chakra system. There are several reasons for such great popularity of this chakra. Humankind has always been fascinated by mysticism. It fears but feels drawn to what it cannot control or command. The powers of the third eye chakra are also of such nature. We will also discuss this chakra in greater detail in order to clear some confusion and explain the reasons for the popularity of this chakra.

First of all, people feel drawn towards this chakra as it can help in increasing the psychic powers of the person who has an active third eye chakra. Here, people have some great misconceptions about the activation of the third eye chakra. Activation of the third eye chakra is not a very difficult task. If your third eye chakra is blocked, you can reopen or reactivate it through correct diet, meditation, and with the help of a person who has an active third eye chakra, etc.

This doesn't take very long or isn't a very difficult thing to do. People simply keep running after the ways to activate this chakra. The important part is to handle it once it gets activated. The third eye chakra is not the door of your safe or refrigerator that can be opened and closed at will. Once it opens up, it will remain open for some time and would require an equal amount of effort, if not more, to close it. However, once it opens up, there is no way for you to escape the powers that come with this chakra,and believe me, for 99% of people who open their third eye chakra, this power becomes the real problem.

Gaining psychic power simply just doesn't mean an ability to look into past and future at will. It also means an uncontrollable journey to the areas you don't want to go to. Initially, you will really have no control over the things you could see. Psychic powers are a boon but only for people who have been practicing them for decades and have gained them slowly.

You may have a great liking for chocolate, but would you like to be thrown in a well of hot chocolate from which there is no way to get out.

Another problem is interaction with energies. When your third eye opens up, your sense of perception multiplies hundreds of times over. This means you will be able to feel energies around you. However, this is just one part of the bargain. This also means that the energies around you would also be able to feel you with the same intensity. There can be energies blocked in this world for very long periods with no one to interact with seeking some form of expression. You would become a medium for them. You can't control what kind of energies interact with you, and all of them may not be positive. In fact, most of them may not be positive. Handling this 24X7 can be a very tall order, and I can say this with a great degree of confidence that you wouldn't be prepared to deal with it. Some people may learn to cope with it somehow, but for most people, it can be like living in a perpetual nightmare with no scope of coming out. This is a reason a very high number of such people develop psychological disorders, but such things fail to get a mention.

This power comes at a great price. Your mind doesn't remain yours, at least not for a reasonably long period of time. You may have to deal with a lot. Every power that comes with the activation of the third eye has a similar cost.

I feel it is again very important to reiterate that as we move up the chakra ladder, the experiential intensity increases manifolds. You may not be ready to deal with that, and hence moving without preparation can be similar to deathwish.

Last but not least, the third eye chakra brings with itself a feeling of complete or utter detachment from this world. A person with an open and active third eye would have no interest in the attractions of this world. This chakra opens the doors of intellectual and spiritual liberation and higher consciousness. It means as soon as this chakra becomes fully-functional, all your desires to gain any kind of material or monetary benefits would go away. Your primary objective would become to find answers to the most complex and important questions concerning this world and life.

Does that mean you shouldn't pursue third eye chakra?

I didn't mean to say that at all. The third eye chakra is the second most powerful chakra in the 7 chakra system. In fact, as per the Vedas, it is the last chakra which you can activate by your will and practice. It is a chakra that will open the doors of higher consciousness. It can help you in getting connected to got, and you will get answers to the questions you have been seeking answers forever. You should most definitely work towards opening this chakra; I only mean to say that opening this chakra without preparation or balancing other chakras shouldn't be done. The second thing, when you try to open this chakra, gaining psychic powers shouldn't be your end goal. You must remain assured that they will automatically come as a byproduct you wish for them or not. Your focus should remain on becoming an able carrier of those powers as and when they arrive.

The third eye chakra stands at the deep end, about which people don't know much and don't even have the resources to find out. Even if a person who has his/her third eye open tells you about a personal experience, that would mean little to you as your experience might be totally different. You might be dealing with a completely different type of energy. All this can leave you in complete shock and even beyond the point of recovery.

So, the pertinent question is:

What is the Best Way to BEGIN Third Eye Activation?

- Always start from the start.
- Do not jump the steps.
- Pay attention to every step

- Ensure that all other chakras in your body are in sync
- Especially work very hard on your root chakra. A weak root chakra can leave you really scared and delusional. Your mind may get filled with fears that would be very hard to deal with.
- Ensure that your heart chakra is working very well. The poorly balanced heart chakra can also cause fears.
- Give almost an equal amount of time to your throat chakra as you have given to all the lower chakras combined. This chakra can enable you to hold such an amount of energy properly.
- Keep your mind and heart pure when you start working on the third eye chakra.
- Do not have negative things in your mind as they can start getting multiplied.
- Only think of the positive things and wish well for everyone.
- Do not wish or think anything bad even for your worst enemy.
- Do not take any shortcut to open your third eye chakra
- Meditation is the best way to open the third eye chakra
- It is also the longest way as it takes a lot of time
- However, it gives your mind the required stability and contentment
- It purifies your emotions and calms you down

- Meditation also removes fear from your heart and mind

One VERY IMPORTANT Point

- Do notPush Your Luck Very Hard
- Let things happen on their own at their own pace

You might have noticed that most of the established psychics gained their powers by accident. They didn't do anything initially to get those powers. For most of them, it happened as a freak accident. Because it came as an accident, they didn't have expectations from it, and hence most of them survive. However, even they face problems initially. But, when you are trying to gain these powers, you are invariably thinking about the use of these powers, and this very thought can become the cause of the whole problem.

The third eye chakra can open anytime in adolescence. We all have it open to some degree. The sixth sense we all have that alerts us about perceived threats is a feature of this third eye chakra. Due to several reasons, this chakra can get blocked, and you may even have to keep working on it constantly to keep it open. Déjà vu, premonitions, gut feelings, and the sixth sense, all are the names of the smaller powers that come with the opening of the third eye chakra. It can also open up on its own in times of danger.

The third eye is not a physical eye. It is an all-seeing eye that opens inwards.

Hinduism represents this third eye as a physical eye on the forehead of shiva. It is believed to the powerful enough to destroy the world if the lord Shiva chooses to open it outwards.

(Image of Hindu Deity Shiva with a physical Third Eye carved in the center of the forehead sitting in a meditative pose.)

The third eye gives a higher sense of perception and clear-sightedness. It may bring with it powers like telepathy, insight, psychic abilities, and higher consciousness. A person with an open third eye will have the realization of his or her full potential. It will increase mental abilities like memory, sharpness, attention, and focus.

The Sanskrit meaning of the word 'Ajna' is 'to command.' This chakra has the ability to command various functions of the body. Because this chakra is the second-highest in the order of 7 chakras, it has greater influence over other chakras. An imbalance in this chakra can cause big problems.

However, until this chakra remains closed, it doesn't cause much harm to anyone. It is only when the energy balance in an active third eye chakra gets disturbed that problems begin.

Balanced Third Eye Chakra: This is the chakra of complete detachment. Once this chakra really opens up in someone, it will take away all the feelings of attachment to this world. This is the chakra of higher consciousness and opens the doors of intellectual and spiritual liberation. Liberation and attachment can't go hand-in-hand. This chakra will take away all kinds of fears from your heart and mind. Even the fear of death wouldn't mean much as it would make the distinction between life and death clear. It raises your cosmic consciousness. This chakra will definitely make you charismatic.

Weak Third Eye Chakra: A weak third eye chakra can make you indecisive, undisciplined, non-assertive, fearful or successes or failures, weak-willed, touchy, paranoid, and even schizophrenic.

Overactive Third Eye Chakra: Excessive energy in this chakra can make a person dogmatic, tyrannical, proud, fundamentalist, or fanatic.

Health Issues Related to Third Eye Chakra: Neurological disturbances, psychosis, seizures, brindles/deafness, and stroke can be seen in people with imbalances in this chakra.

The Crown Chakra

This is the seventh chakra in the system of 7 chakras and the topmost in order. There are some very interesting things about this chakra. It is full of mysteries and mysticism.

The meaning of the Sanskrit word 'Sahasrara' means a thousand petals. However, if you consider it in terms of 1000's of years old writing, it would mean countless petals. On this level of chakra, everything is simply speculation.

The Vedas have explained several ways to reach from the 1st chakra to the 6th chakra, but there is no specific way to reach or open the 7th chakra. To open this chakra, no specific way has been told.

Does this mean that this chakra can't be opened or activated?

Definitely not. In fact, many sages have given accounts where they were able to activate and achieve this chakra and consciousness. They simply said that it is impossible to explain the path to open it. From the sixth chakra to the seventh, there is no path. In the words of the acclaimed teacher and spiritual master SadhguruJaggi Vasudev, from the sixth chakra to the seventh chakra, it is a pathless path. One has to find his/her own path through the power of acquired intellectual and spiritual consciousness.

Vedas state that at the 6th chakra, you will have achieved everything you would have wanted to achieve. There is nothing in terms of attainment that you could get at the 7th chakra. This chakra doesn't come with mystical powers that charm people. It is simply a door to endless and rare knowledge about higher consciousness and liberation. It is a path on which there is no surety of return. Once you reach there, you may not want to return, or the return may become futile. Once you know what's there, knowing or seeing anything else may become completely inconsequential. It is a certain path of complete detachment.

Sahasrara means thousands of petals or unlimited magnitude. These unlimited petals are the doors of knowledge. These are doors or ways of liberation. In the Hindu religion, peace is not the ultimate goal of humankind. Vedas say that the ultimate goal is to gain liberation from this cycle of birth and death. The goal of expanding human consciousness is to solve the broader questions of the universe. People believe that once this chakra completely opens up, knowing anything becomes easy. Your consciousness and the consciousness of the universe become one at this point.

People have tried for centuries and have come up with certain guidelines that may help in opening up this chakra.

This chakra is simply a way to connect to the divine force. Even in Vedas, the seventh chakra is not described as a medium to meet any god or deity. It is simply described as a way to unite with the divine force in whatever form it may come. The journey to the seventh chakra is in no way intellectual or religious; it is purely spiritual.

However, you must become cautious that this is the most powerful chakra of all. The amount of energy at this level may become very difficult for anyone to handle if this path opens up accidentally.

The Vedas place the physical location of all the remaining six chakras within our body; this is the only chakra that's said to be located outside our body. The physical location of this chakra is said to be around six inches above the center of our skull. This chakra is outside our body and yet influences us very strongly. Therefore, while moving towards this chakra, one must remain cautious.

Balanced Crown Chakra: Balanced energy in the crown chakra can help you establish a connection with the divine. It can set you on the path of liberation, which is the goal of opening this chakra. It may give you direct access to the unconscious, as well as the subconscious. People speculate that even the basic laws of nature may not matter at this level. You will gain complete awareness about death, and it would become inconsequential for you. Some also like to believe that a person with an open and active crown chakra may be able to do things that maybe miracles for the common people.

Weak Crown Chakra: Although we have little knowledge about the things that can be achieved after unlocking the crown chakra, the dangers of energy imbalance are well known. If the energies are weak in this chakra, it can make a person feel completely dejected. That person may experience a complete lack of joy and may also become uncommunicative. Becoming catatonic is also a possibility some people predict. However, such a person would definitely face problems in making decisions as it affects the cognitive abilities required to discern between good and bad or right and wrong.

Overactive Crown Chakra: Excessive energies in this chakra can leave a person highly frustrated. The level of intensity at this level is so high that you wouldn't want to mess with it. You may feel that you have unrealized power but wouldn't know a way to discover it, and this may cause more frustration. Frequent migraine headaches, destructive tendencies, maniac-suppressive disorder to psychotic behavior, the list of problems can be far and wide.

Health Issues Related to Crown Chakra: Problems in this chakra can lead to cognitive disorders. Mystical depression, extreme sensitivity to light, sound, and environment, and diseases of the muscular system are some of the problems that can arise due to an imbalance of the energies in this chakra.

Chapter 7: The Reasons for Chakra Blockage or Imbalance and Ways in Which It Affects Your Life

Chakras are subtle energy bodies. The seven chakras as we know them aren't inside our body, and hence they really don't get blocked. However, every major chakra represents 16 minor chakras that are present inside the body. It is the blockage in those chakras that leads to overall energy blockage.

For the sake of developing a clear understanding, it is very important that you understand the cause of the blockage. Before that, it is also important that you understand 'energy' clearly.

All energy systems believe it unanimously that there is a certain force that flows inside and keeps us running. This energy is known by several names like Chi, Qui, or Ki. In the *IndianPranic* system, this energy is known as the *'Prana'* or life force.

Vedas say that out of millions of nerves; there are 72000 main nerves that facilitate the flow of this prana throughout the body. This prana flows through these nerves at 112 crucial junctions in the body, and these junctions are known as 'chakras.' These chakras are very important as they directly influence the flow of physical, emotional, intellectual, and spiritual energy inside the body.

However, as they influence the flow of these energies, these chakras can also get affected by various physical, emotional, and mental and spiritual pressures.

Therefore, the flow of *pranic* energy in your body or *prana* can get affected due to emotional, physical, and mental issues. The chakras have a strong influence on these areas, but the physical aspect of the chakras can also get affected by them.

It is possible for any chakra to get clogged physically. If your body gets physically impaired in any way, it will lead to clogging up of the chakras as the flow of *prana* will get affected. The *prana* is subtle energy flowing in your body, just like the blood flows through your veins.

If your mind is disturbed, it will also obstruct the flow of this subtle energy. The *prana* in such cases gets more focused on resolving the mental issues, and its flow gets affected. Similarly, emotional issues also have a very strong impact on the smooth flow of *prana* in the body.

Therefore, if you are suffering from some chronic illness or have been in constant physical pain, it will have a deep impact on this flow of *pranic* energy. It is a very natural thing to happen. The Vedic tradition believes in resolving the cause and not treating the symptom. If you start your mission to correct your chakras in this stage, you'll have very little success even after very hard work. The reason is simple; the cause of chakra blockage in your body would remain unaffected. You will have to address the physical issue first.

Major reasons for chakra blockage are, however, emotional rather than physical. Some of the common problems that cause chakra blockage or energy imbalance in the chakras are:

- Unresolved Emotional Issues
- Long-held Resentments
- Inability to Release Negative Emotions or Inability to Find Outlet
- Stress
- Anxiety
- Fear
- Programming faced While Being Raised
- Self-Imposed Restriction
- Abuse
- Past Traumatic Events
- Repressed Emotions
- Undue Stress on the Mother while the Child was still Unborn

The last point may look strange, but you'd be astonished to know the number of people who have blocked chakras because their mothers were under great stress when they were still in their womb. This is among the chief reasons expecting mothers are highly advised to remain stress-free and happy. Their emotional and mental state is going to affect their kids directly.

Another chief reason for the blockage in the chakras is our habit of putting our little joys for tomorrow. While we struggle in our education, jobs, and careers, we set a later date for being happy. You might know some people who say that they'll enjoy it when they retire and therefore, they work more than they should in the present. They put all their happiness at stake. Kids mortgage their present happiness at stake for a time when they pass victoriously. All these things lead to repressed emotions. We don't realize, but these things put pressure on our *pranic* energy.

The blood flows in your veins continuously. You can't put it off for tomorrow. You continuously need to breathe and inhale *Prana Vayu* or air. You can't put it off for a later date. Similarly, the *prana* also flows continuously and can't be put on hold. However, there is a big difference between blood and *prana*. The blood is fluid and physical, and it has a mechanism to push it at a constant rate, whereas the *prana* is energy. The flow of your energy will depend on your mental and emotional state. If you are feeling happy and stable, the flow of energy would be good and strong as the energy would be excited. However, when there are a lot of repressed emotions, stress, anxiety, and sorrow, this *pranic* energy would get low, and the flow would get poor. This will cause low energy.

The reason we only focus on 7 main chakras and not the minor 112 chakras is this only. You will have no system to understand which chakra is facing low energy and would have no mechanism to address that chakra in a timely and effective manner.

The 7 major chakras are connected to the 112 chakras through the endocrine glands. The endocrine glands are ductless glands in means they have the ability to influence bodily functions through chemical messengers called hormones. These 7 chakras also influence the crucial nerve centers that are connected to the 112 minor chakras.

The seven major chakra points simply act as acupressure points in your body that can help in bringing this change in motion.

There are several things you can do to prevent blockage of chakras or to minimize the chances of such blockages:

- Try to remain joyful
- Live in the present, don't put off your happiness for tomorrow
- Try to address unresolved emotional issues as early as possible
- Do not hold grudges against others, if you can't do anything else, forgive them and move on

- Do not get stuck on things. It takes away a lot of *pranic*energy
- Try to release as much negative energy as possible
- Do meditation regularly; it will help you in addressing most of these issues
- Do yoga or other such exercises
- Remain physically active
- Get treatment for physical issues and don't ignore chronic pain
- Take steps to lower stress and anxiety in your life
- Seek help to address past traumatic events in your life
- Get over your past
- Learn to let go and move on as fast as possible
- Try to bring joy in the life of others, the positive energy and blessings of others can help a lot in bringing balance in your pranic energy

Chakra blockage is an energy disturbance, and it can happen due to a number of reasons. There is no use fretting over split milk in life. The important thing to do is to address those issues and restore the balance of energy in life.

Most of us keep blaming others for the problems we have. We forget that the pain we endure is not being caused by them but due to the grudge that we hold against them. We stop trying to get over that pain or discomfort as we want to hold that grudge or increase its intensity. It is going to hurt us even more and wouldn't affect that person even a bit.

It is very important to learn the art of forgiving and moving on. The chakra energy is real, and it has physical manifestations. As long as you keep treating it as a mythical concept, you will not be able to get its benefits. Try to see it in real and practical terms, and everything about the chakras would turn out to be true.

Chapter 8: Meaning of Chakra Balancing and Awakening

Chakra balancing and awakening are two different things. There is a lot of confusion about both the concepts, and they are usually mixed up and even used interchangeably. This chapter will help you in clearing the confusion.

There are several states in which the Chakras can be in your body:

Open Chakras: Six chakras out of the seven open up in your body with time. It is a natural process. There is a set age for the opening up of the chakras.

No.	Chakra	Orientation	Central Issue	Identity	Age
1	Root Chakra	Self-Preservation	Survival	Physical Identity	Up to 1 Year
2	Sacral Chakra	Self-Gratification	Sexuality	Emotional Identity	Up to 2 Years
3	Solar Plexus Chakra	Self-Definition	Power	Ego Identity	Up to 5 Years

4	Heart Chakra	Self-Acceptance	Love	Social Identity	Up to 8 Years
5	Throat Chakra	Self-Expression	Communication	Creative Identity	Up to 12 Years
6	Third Eye Chakra	Self-Reflection	Intuition	Archetypal Identity	Adolescence
7	Crown Chakra	Self-Knowledge	Awareness	Universal Identity	On Experience

Therefore, you will see that six out of seven chakras have their set time to open up. The age given in the table above is the age of development of this chakra or energy system. From this age, the system becomes functional. This means that if you want to work on the throat chakra at the age of 4, you may not get great success. It is not impossible to open up this chakra sooner, but the optimum age of development of a specific chakra is given. Only the seventh chakra doesn't have a specific age of development. It is an experiential chakra, and it is always present there. You will have to reach that level of consciousness to open it up.

Active Chakras: Another major concern is about chakras being active. An active chakra is the one through which a steady and healthy flow of energy transfer takes place. This generally happens in most of the chakra until they get blocked due to any specific reason. However, the chakras may not be transferring energy very actively. With time, stress, repressed emotions, the level of energy transfer goes down. To be considered a chakra active, it must have the optimum level of energy transfer taking place. Even clogged chakras facilitate some degree of energy transfer. That doesn't really make them active. An active chakra is the one through which the transfer of energy is taking place swiftly.

Awakening Chakras: It is the process of restoring the energy flow in a chakra. When a chakra has been dormant for a very long time, the process of making it active is known as awakening.

Blocked/Clogged Chakras: Blocked or clogged chakras are those in which the energy flow is not taking place properly. Chakras can get blocked or clogged due to a number of reasons. Emotional, mental, and physical issues can lead to chakra blocking/clogging. Such problems can be resolved through chakra balancing.

Healing/Balancing Chakras: Chakra healing is the process of restoring the energy balance in a chakra. There can be several ways employed to heal/balance chakras.

- Meditation is a good way to restore the energy balance in the chakras.
- You can also do this through yoga, ti-chi, or other such methods.
- Crystals and essential oils can also help in restoring the energy flow and healing a slow functioning chakra.
- Reiki is another way to kick start the flow of energy in a chakra.
- Bringing some positive changes in your lifestyle is also a good way to restore and maintain the balance of the chakras

The energy balance of the chakras gets influenced by your day to day actions and thought processes. You may not know but the things you are having in mind or the actions you perform affect the flow of *Prana Vayu* or life energy in your body you can also consider it an equivalent of breathing. For instance, when you are excited, your breathing becomes rapid, this changes the way *prana* flows through your nervous system. Similarly, if you are very calm and relaxed, your breathing would get very deep, there will be no tension in the nerves, and there would be no need to direct the *prana* to any specific part of the body. Hence, the flow of the *prana* would be smooth. Therefore, our day to day thoughts and actions have a deep impact on the chakras. If you want to maintain a smooth flow of energy, you can follow some simple habits to keep your chakras aligned.

The next few chapters will help you in understanding in detail the ways to heal your chakras. You will also get daily life tips to heal your blocked chakras.

This book will cover 5 easy and effective ways to heal the chakras and keep them balanced.

1. Yoga Asanas (Yoga Postures)
2. Crystals to heal the chakras and the ways to use them
3. Essential oils for healing the blocked chakras
4. Daily Life Tips for restoring and maintaining energy balance
5. Meditation- This book will give you individual guided meditation sessions for healing and balancing each chakra

Additionally, this book will also cover Reiki briefly as you can also take the help of Reiki healers for opening your blocked chakras instantly or restoring the energy balance.

Chapter 9: Methods of Chakra Healing and Balancing

1. Meditation

Meditation is one of the most accurate ways to heal and balance your chakras. Vedas lay a great deal of emphasis on meditation. Unlike the western world, the Vedas don't see meditation as a way to calm the mind or settle down the mind chatter. Vedas consider mediation as the most concrete way to connect to your inner consciousness. With the help of meditation, you can build a razor-sharp focus and pinpoint your energies to the specific areas where it is needed. There is no other way to heal and balance the chakras so accurately.

Meditation is considered to be a superior medium for several reasons.

First, it is an internal process to channelize energy. It doesn't require any outside help.

Second, it brings the changes gradually, and hence your energy centers get appropriate time to adjust. There is no sudden and swift change of energy, which can be a cause of concern at times.

Third, Meditation increases your focus on your subtle energies and the energy centers. This also prevents frequent blockages.

Fourth, the chakras have a very delicate energy balance. The external mediums used to heal the chakras can also cause more damage as there is no way to judge the exact amount of energy push required. It usually works on a trial and error basis through external mediums, and your guess could be as right as mine. However, meditation brings the changes in a very subtle manner without causing any disturbance to the energy flow of other chakras.

Fifth, it is a healthy practice to keep your body and mind in sync. It calms your mind and also soothes your emotions. By practicing meditation, you will be able to give an outlet to your repressed emotions. Letting go of past memories and regressive thoughts also become easier.

The benefits of using meditation are plenty.

2. Yoga

To the western world, yoga is primarily a way to remain physically and mentally fit. However, the Indian *Pranic*system or the Vedic system considered it much more.

In the Vedic system, the Yoga has 8 arms.

1. Yama (Moral Codes)
2. Niyama (Self-Purification and Study)
3. Asana (Posture)
4. Pranayama (Breath Control)
5. Pratyahara (Sense Control)
6. Dharana (Concentration)
7. Dhyana (Meditation)
8. Samadhi (Assimilation with the Universal Energy)

As you can see, the first four parts are about controlling the body and the mind. They address the issues that are faced by the body. Through various postures, breath control, and self-purification, you make your body healthy and fit. These things give you the power to keep your body aligned.

The rest of the four parts of yoga are not physical but more concerned about mental and emotional development. As you can see here, the 7th part of yoga is meditation. So, both yoga and meditation are used for the same goal. They are part of the same sequence. As you can see, even in Yoga, the ultimate goal is to get one with the universal energy. In the Vedic culture, all parts ultimately lead to one goal, and that is the final liberation of the body, mind, and spirit.

However, in yoga, there are specific asanas or postures that can help you in putting the right pressure on the required chakras. You can also do yoga to keep your chakras well.

3. Crystal Healing

Crystal healing is a simple way of healing the energy imbalance by using stones. You may wonder, how can a stone, an inanimate object correct an energy balance inside the body. It may look like a superstition.

Now, think of uranium. It is also an inanimate object, yet, if you stay close to it, you can get irreparable damage to your body and your mind. You don't even need to touch it or come in direct contact with it. You may simply answer that it is a radioactive material, and that's why it affects us. Radioactive nature is also a form of energy. Every object in this world has its energy. The energy is usually very subtle, and we can't feel it. However, the subtle energy centers in our body can feel this energy, and by using these stones, you can help in restoring the energy balance. If there are chakras with low energy, you can use crystals that can empower those chakras and help restore the balance.

Similarly, in the case of overactive chakras, crystals can be used which absorb that kind of energy.

However, before you handle any crystal, it is important that you ensure that the crystals are of the right type and quality. Using inferior crystals may not have any impact on your energy levels. This doesn't mean that you have to buy costly crystals like a diamond. You can use affordable alternatives, but the crystals used shouldn't be inferior or broken. If a stone turns pale over a period of time, please change that stone.

Before you start using any kind of crystal, it is important that you clear them for any kind of residual energy. You will certainly not be the first person to handle the crystal which you would be using. This means that the crystal would have come in contact with several people in the past. Crystals can retain energies for a very long period, and that may work against you as the energies retained by the crystals may also be negative. To ensure that this doesn't affect you, please clean the crystals carefully before using them.

There are some very easy ways to clean the crystals:

- Wash them under running tap water. Keeping them under flowing tap water of around 15 minutes can remove negative energies

- You can simply keep the crystals under the moonlight for 3 nights consecutively. But, ensure that they do not come in contact with sunlight as it can damage some crystals.
- Keep them in a bowl of sea-salt. This will also remove negative energies. Wash them with fresh water after taking them out of sea-salt.
- You can also bury crystals in the ground at night and take out the next morning to remove negative energies.

Keeping the stones close to your body or keeping it exactly on the affected chakra location can help in healing the chakra faster.

4. Essential Oils

Ayurveda, the branch of Vedic medicine followed in ancient India, played a lot of emphasis on plants in our health. It states that there are several plants that have strong medicative use in our lives. Using those plants in various forms can help in treating problems of various types.

Healing energy imbalance in the chakras is also one among them. There are many exotic plants that produce certain herbs that can influence the energy levels in your body. Extracts from such plants can be used in the form of essential oils to treat many types of energy imbalances.

There are many popular ways to use essential oils. You can mix the essential oil in any carrier oil and apply it directly to your skin in the affected area. This can help in restoring the energy balance.

These essential oils can also be used for aromatherapy, where it is used in incense sticks for soothing your sense through fragrance.

5. Lifestyle Changes

Our actions affect the way our energy system works. The easiest way to understand is to know Newton's 3rd law of motion. It says that every action has an equal and opposite reaction.

When you scold a person or get angry with someone, you are not only causing hurt and pain to that person, but your internal mechanism is also getting affected by the scorn of yourself. You don't remain unaffected by this explosion of energy. It is a natural reaction. Similarly, if you smile after looking at someone, show affection, or do some kind deed for others, you will see a softness of emotion developing inside. This is simply a reaction of the kind deed. All this is to prove that every action in life will affect your chakras.

For instance, if you have a habit of lying too much or you are a habitual liar, your throat chakra will always be out of balance. It can make you even more talkative as that is the side effect of excessive energy in this chakra, but that doesn't make it good. The best way to bring balance to the overactive throat chakra is to stop lying compulsively.

Similarly, there are many simple ways to keep the chakras in balance. You wouldn't need a lot of effort to do that. So, if you know the chakra with an imbalance in your life, you can start following those tips.

6. Reiki

Reiki is a powerful Japanese healing technique that works on similar energy principles. In this technique, a trained Reiki master who has developed healing powers can help you by finding and healing the energy imbalance in the body.

Reiki masters are trained extensively to detect the obstruction in the flow of energy, and they use it for healing problems. If you are facing any problem in your energy centers, you can take the help of Reiki masters. As I have stated earlier, this help should not be taken to activate the third eye chakra spontaneously, as managing its energy can become difficult for you.

Chapter 10: Chakra Healing and Balancing

Root Chakra Healing

Lifestyle Changes for Root Chakra Healing and Balancing

Make Gardening a Hobby

To restore balance in the root chakra, you can begin gardening. The more you interact with the soil, the stronger your root chakra will become. This hobby can help in keeping your mind disengaged and would also help in alleviating your fears. Practice gardening daily for at least some time. Even if you live in a metropolitan city with tight constraints of space, keeping flowerpots is still an option you can follow. You can also try keeping one indoor plant even on your work desk for a better grounding effect.

Earth Sitting and Hiking

Try to establish as close a connection with the earth as you can. The imbalance in the root chakra is usually a result of disassociation from the roots. People going far away from their homes also face this disturbance. You can try sitting on the ground for some time every day in the parks. Hiking trips are also a good idea as they help you in maintaining a close connection with nature.

Come in Contact with the Ground

There are several ways in which you can establish contact with the ground. Walking barefoot on the ground is also a great idea. In fact, it is even considered very good for the health of the eyes to walk barefoot on the grass. However, it is also good for bringing a balance in the root chakra.

Get Out of a Sedentary Lifestyle

There is no doubt in the fact that the modern lifestyle has a great role to play in our sedentary lifestyles. However, even our contribution to the problem is no less. We have become couch potatoes and don't take the initiative. If your root chakra is out of balance, try to do more physical activity. Remember that an imbalanced root chakra can also increase your weight unexpectedly.

Red Fruits are Good

Eating red fruits is good for bringing a balance in the root chakra.

Yoga for Root Chakra Healing and Balancing

- Tree Pose
- Standing Forward Bend
- Head to Knee Pose
- Supported Child's Pose
- Supported Corpse Pose
- Warrior 1
- Warrior 2
- Chair Pose

Crystals for Root Chakra Healing and Balancing

Ruby, bloodstone, hematite, obsidian, red jasper, onyx, lodestone, fire agate, garnet, black tourmaline, and smoky quartz.

Essential Oils for Root Chakra Healing and Balancing

Rosewood, sandalwood, and ylang-ylang

Root Chakra Healing Meditation

Sit in a cross-legged posture

Close your eyes gently

Keep your spine upright

If you feel the need, you can use a backrest

Please maintain an upright posture throughout the meditation session

Keep your shoulders straight and equidistant

Your next should also remain straight

Please raise your chin a little upwards towards the sky

Just a little bit

You can place your hands in your lap or on your lap as you feel comfortable

During the course of the meditation, you will need to keep your eyes closed

You may get several thoughts related to your personal and professional thoughts during the meditation

Do not pay attention to them

Simply push them aside and pay attention to your breathing

Your focus should be on your awareness

This meditation session will help you in establishing a strong connection to your roots. It will help make you feel more grounded and firm. The feeling of contentment, self-sufficiency, and peace, which are missing, would become stronger in your heart after this session.

Sit calmly with your eyes gently closed

You don't need to think anything at this moment

This is the time to relax

If there are thoughts rushing to your mind, don't worry

Let them pass

They don't concern you at the moment

You are to become a calm and peaceful person at this moment

No need to think about anything

No need to focus on sorrow or happiness

No need to worry about failures and success

No need to worry about fears of pleasures

This is the moment to remain still and silent

You don't need to do anything

Bring your awareness on your breathing

Observe your breathing closely

Inhale

Exhale

Inhale

Exhale

Inhale

Exhale

Inhale

Exhale

Inhale

Exhale

Keep your focus glued to your breathing

Try to feel every aspect of your breathing

Is your breathing rapid at the moment?

It will cool down.

Is the air cold or warm?

Can you sense the air entering your nostrils?

Pay attention to this air

We will now do deep breathing

You will inhale slowly through your nose to my count of 7

Hold it to the count of 7

Then exhale very slowly through your mouth to the count of 8

Maintain your focus on the breath

Don't let it wander away

It may get diverted to some random thoughts

Do not worry

Simply acknowledge the thought and bring your attention back to breathing

Take a slow and deep breath through your nose

1..

2...

3....

4.....

5....

6......

7......

Now gently hold this breath to the count of 7

1..

2...

3....

4.....

5....

6......

7......

Now exhale through your mouth slowly to the count of 8

1..

2...

3....

4.....

5....

6......

7......

8.......

Excellent!

Repeat once again

Take a slow and deep breath through your nose

1..

2...

3....

4.....

5....

6......

7......

Now gently hold this breath to the count of 7

1..

2...

3....

4.....

5....

6......

7......

Now exhale through your mouth slowly to the count of 8

1..

2...

3....

4.....

5....

6......

7......

8.......

Wonderful!!

Observe your breathing once again

Feel the calm in your breathing now

Now, once again take a deep breath

No need to count

Simply breath deeply for as long as you can

Let your body soak in as much fresh air as it can

While you inhale,

Let your awareness follow this air inside your body

Feel this air entering your nasal cavity

Observe the way this breath inflates your chest and moves downward

Direct it to the base of your spine through your awareness

Let it reach to the core

The base of the spine is the core of the body

Like there is a core to the earth

Feel your core of the body getting connected to the core of the earth

Keep breathing slowly

Inhale

Exhale

Inhale

Exhale

Feel your core getting connected to the mother earth

You are made from that same earth

One day you will get dissolved in this earth

You are not going to lose anything

There is nothing that you need to fear

There is nothing that should bother you

You get everything from this mother earth

Everything gets back to the earth

You are satisfied with whatever you have

You feel content with what you own

You feel connected to your roots

You feel a strong bond with the family

You feel safe and secure

You are feeling warm and snug

You are feeling at home

You have come here to be here

You have the right to have the things you own

You are feeling light

You are feeling strong

Inhale

Exhale

Inhale

Exhale

Feel the calm, soothing energy prevailing over your body

Visualize the soothing warm red light coming out of the earth and warming your body

It is the love, care, and protection provided by the mother earth

You are feeling confident now

You are feeling calm

You are feeling safe

The earth is the mother

It nurtures you

It provides protection to you

It wouldn't allow any harm come to you

Feel yourself getting connected to the mother

Find yourself warmly snuggled into the lap of the mother

You can solve all the problems you have

You are fearless

You are powerful

The mother is nurturing you

It is providing protection to you

Let the mother earth fill you with its warm light

Let it illuminate you from the inside

Just sit still

Feel the power

Feel the calm

Feel the stillness

Feel your insecurities melting away

Feel your fear going away

Now, there is no fear

There is no anxiety

You are feeling safe and secure

You are feeling grounded and nourished

You are feeling connected to the mother earth

You are feeling connected to the family

Accept whatever you receive

There are no questions to ask

There are no answers to give

Please receive from the eternal mother

Let the mother nourish you

Inhale slowly

Exhale even slower

Inhale slowly

Exhale even slower

Inhale slowly

Exhale even slower

Now shift your focus to your breathing again

You are feeling positive now

You are feeling healed and nourished

Inhale

Exhale

Inhale

Exhale

Inhale

Exhale

Bring your focus back to breathing

Feel your breath once again

Try to feel your surrounding

Try to feel your limbs without moving them

Relax

Sit for a few moments with your eyes closed

Now, you can open your eyes whenever you wish

Sacral Chakra Healing

Lifestyle Changes for Sacral Chakra Healing and Balancing

Increase Your Creative Engagement

This is the chakra that encourages creative pursuits. It makes you feel and taste new things and gives way to your creativity. However, when the energy in this chakra is low, doing new things or engaging in creative pursuits can help in restoring the balance in this chakra.

Go to New Places

New places can create excitement in this chakra as it is given to the pleasure of new and unknown things and places. If your sacral chakra is low on energy, visiting new places can titillate your visual experience and in turn, help in improving this chakra's functioning.

Try New Food Items

Taste, smell, and visual experience are among the three strong senses. Tasting new dishes and trying new foods can also have a positive impact on your sacral chakra. This can arouse your interest in the things around you.

Dedicate Some Time to Social Service

Social service is another way to create interest in the things around you. Although the sacral chakra is about enjoying the pleasures of the world, when the energies in this chakra are low, spreading some joy around, you can also bring positive energy to this chakra. You should try doing some community service in any way possible. No service is too small for humanity. You don't need to become a big philanthropist for doing social work. Try to contribute in any which way possible.

Find Proper Outlet for Your Sexual Energy

This is the chakra that has a direct influence over your reproductive organs. It is also a chakra just above the root chakra, and hence the buildup of sexual energy in this chakra shouldn't be considered something very unusual. However, sexual energy should be given a proper outlet. If let out of control, this chakra can make you completely devoted to sexual pleasures, and only carnal desires would start dictating your decisions. Engaging in unlawful sexual activities or adultery can cause another set of issues in this chakra. It leads to the buildup of negative emotions, and that can be harmful to you. Try to find a proper outlet for your sexual gratification.

Try Reiki

Reiki can be very helpful in resolving problems in this chakra. Because this chakra lies in the lower rungs and its impact is primarily inwards, you can easily consult a reiki master for the healing of this chakra. A reiki master can correct the issues comparatively faster.

Wear Orange Color

Orange color clothes and food of orange color can b helpful in restoring the balance in this chakra. Colors have a deep impact on your sense, and that's why wearing this chakra will motivate you to become a bit more immersive.

Yoga for Sacral Chakra Healing and Balancing

- Four limb staff pose
- Downward facing dog
- Cow face pose
- Child's pose
- Happy baby pose
- Warrior poses
- Bound angle pose
- Open-angle pose

Crystals for Sacral Chakra Healing and Balancing

Amber, moonstone, sunstone, orange tourmaline, and carnelian

Essential Oils for Sacral Chakra Healing and Balancing

Rosewood, lemon, lavender, and rosemary, and roman chamomile

Sacral Chakra Healing Meditation

Sit in a cross-legged posture

Close your eyes gently

Keep your spine upright

If you feel the need, you can use a backrest

Please maintain an upright posture throughout the meditation session

Keep your shoulders straight and equidistant

Your next should also remain straight

Please raise your chin a little upwards towards the sky

Just a little bit

You can place your hands in your lap or on your lap as you feel comfortable

During the course of the meditation, you will need to keep your eyes closed

You may get several thoughts related to your personal and professional thoughts during the meditation

Do not pay attention to them

Simply push them aside and pay attention to your breathing

Your focus should be on your awareness

This meditation session will help you in rekindling your childlike spirit. You will find that joy is still a fresh and fulfilling feeling. This meditation session will help you in exploring the joyful side of your personality. It will help you in exploring your passions and rediscovering the old you that you have been missing for long or have always desired.

Sit calmly with your eyes gently closed

You don't need to think anything at this moment

This is the time to relax

If there are thoughts rushing to your mind, don't worry

Let them pass

They don't concern you at the moment

You are to become a calm and peaceful person at this moment

No need to think about anything

No need to focus on sorrow or happiness

No need to worry about failures and success

No need to worry about fears of pleasures

This is the moment to remain still and silent

You don't need to do anything

Bring your awareness on your breathing

Observe your breathing closely

Inhale

Exhale

Inhale

Exhale

Inhale

Exhale

Inhale

Exhale

Inhale

Exhale

Keep your focus glued to your breathing

Try to feel every aspect of your breathing

Is your breathing rapid at the moment?

It will cool down.

Is the air cold or warm?

Can you sense the air entering your nostrils?

Pay attention to this air

We will now do deep breathing

You will inhale slowly through your nose to my count of 7

Hold it to the count of 7

Then exhale very slowly through your mouth to the count of 8

Maintain your focus on the breath

Don't let it wander away

It may get diverted to some random thoughts

Do not worry

Simply acknowledge the thought and bring your attention back to breathing

Take a slow and deep breath through your nose

1..

2...

3....

4.....

5....

6......

7......

Now gently hold this breath to the count of 7

1..

2...

3....

4.....

5....

6......

7......

Now exhale through your mouth slowly to the count of 8

1..

2...

3....

4.....

5....

6......

7......

8.......

Excellent!

Repeat once again

Take a slow and deep breath through your nose

1..

2...

3....

4.....

5....

6......

7......

Now gently hold this breath to the count of 7

1..

2...

3....

4.....

5....

6......

7......

Now exhale through your mouth slowly to the count of 8

1..

2...

3....

4.....

5....

6......

7……

8…….

Wonderful!!

Observe your breathing once again

Feel the calm in your breathing now

Take a deep breath once again and follow the path it takes

Observe the breath pass through your nostrils

Follow it all the way passing through the lungs

Feel it going towards your navel cavity

Feel it hit the point of the sacral chakra

Isn’t the feeling thrilling?

Repeat the process once again

Take a deep breath once again and follow the path it takes

Observe the breath pass through your nostrils

Follow it all the way passing through the lungs

Feel it going towards your navel cavity

Feel it hit the point of the sacral chakra

It is such an amazing feeling

Feel the orange color light emanating from that point

It is the energy of the sacral chakra

It had got trapped inside the chakra

Feel it spreading all around

Visualize your whole body getting colored in the orange color

It is illuminating you from inside

This is the energy that makes you experience this whole world

It fills you with vigor and vitality

It makes you lively and joyful

You feel the thrill of life inside you

Do you feel the tinge of sexual arousal

There is nothing to be ashamed of this feeling

It is to be enjoyed

Feel the thrill running throughout your body

There is no need to run away from it

Accept it

Absorb it

Drink it

Don't be scared of it

This is your energy

It has always been inside you

You are simply rediscovering yourself once again

Let this orange energy spread to all parts of your body

Let it fill you with vigor and vitality

Inhale

Exhale

Inhale

Exhale

Bring your awareness back to your breathing

Take a deep breath

Inhale

Exhale

Inhale

Exhale

Inhale

Exhale

Keeping your eyes closed observe your breathing closely

Keep your focus on your breathing

Inhale

Exhale

Inhale

Exhale

Bring your focus back to breathing

Feel your breath once again

Try to feel your surrounding

Try to feel your limbs without moving them

Relax

Sit for a few moments with your eyes closed

Now, you can open your eyes whenever you wish

Solar Plexus Chakra Healing

Lifestyle Changes for Solar Plexus Chakra Healing and Balancing

Re-establish Your Connection with the Sun

The solar plexus chakra fills you with the bright light of the Sun and makes you as energetic and powerful as the Sun itself. However, if you are feeling low in this chakra, looking at the soothing light of Sun at dusk and dawn can help in restoring the balance in this chakra. While you Sungaze, please remember not to do it for very long periods and never to look at the Sun for long in the day as it can cause great harm to your eyes.

Do Sunbathing

Sunbathing will also have a similar impact on your life. Sunbathing will help in recharging your solar plexus chakra physically. However, even for sunbathing, you must refrain from doing it for too long in bright sunlight as it can harm your skin.

Maintain Healthy Boundaries

An overactive solar plexus chakra can easily make you cross personal and professional boundaries, and you may appear as a domineering, overly critical, and demanding person. Maintaining healthy relationships in such a scenario can become difficult. To tone down your solar plexus chakra, you must practice healthy boundaries in personal and professional life. The more you keep yourself contained in boundaries, the easier it would become to restore the energy balance.

Break Complescancy

If the energy in this chakra is low, it will stop you from taking risks or coming out of the comfort zone. However, if you don't try, this would keep dragging you down even deeper. The best way out is to try to break free of the comfort zone and take new challenges head-on. The more adventurously you behave, the more energized this chakra would become. This is the chakra of risk-takers and challengers. It gives you the appetite to digest the whole world; you must not think twice before taking a small bite.

Develop a Physically Engaging/Challenging Daily Routine

Become highly active. Dull and boring routine can take energy out of this chakra. Try to do something at least once, which involves intense physical labor as it would keep your batteries charged.

Yellow Fruits and Clothes

Eating yellow fruits and wearing yellow clothes can help in charging this chakra faster. You can also choose to wear gold as that also helps.

Yoga for Solar Plexus Chakra Healing and Balancing

- Half-boat pose
- Sun salutation
- Pranayam or breathing techniques
- Cow pose
- Boat pose
- Cat pose
- Bellows breath

Crystals for Solar Plexus Chakra Healing and Balancing

Yellow topaz, yellow tiger's eye, yellow citrine, amber,rutilated quartz, and yellow agate

Essential Oils for Solar Plexus Chakra Healing and Balancing

Rosewood, lemon, lavender, roman chamomile, and rosemary

Solar Plexus Chakra Healing Meditation

Sit in a cross-legged posture

Close your eyes gently

Keep your spine upright

If you feel the need, you can use a backrest

Please maintain an upright posture throughout the meditation session

Keep your shoulders straight and equidistant

Your next should also remain straight

Please raise your chin a little upwards towards the sky

Just a little bit

You can place your hands in your lap or on your lap as you feel comfortable

During the course of the meditation, you will need to keep your eyes closed

You may get several thoughts related to your personal and professional thoughts during the meditation

Do not pay attention to them

Simply push them aside and pay attention to your breathing

Your focus should be on your awareness

This meditation session will help you in finding your spontaneity, vitality, and will. There are times when all starts to look lost. However, the Sun rises in the east daily and brings with itself new hopes and possibilities. This meditation session will help you in rediscovering your lost hopes, aspirations, and ambitions.

Sit calmly with your eyes gently closed

You don’t need to think anything at this moment

This is the time to relax

If there are thoughts rushing to your mind, don’t worry

Let them pass

They don't concern you at the moment

You are to become a calm and peaceful person at this moment

No need to think about anything

No need to focus on sorrow or happiness

No need to worry about failures and success

No need to worry about fears of pleasures

This is the moment to remain still and silent

You don't need to do anything

Bring your awareness on your breathing

Observe your breathing closely

Inhale

Exhale

Inhale

Exhale

Inhale

Exhale

Inhale

Exhale

Inhale

Exhale

Keep your focus glued to your breathing

Try to feel every aspect of your breathing

Is your breathing rapid at the moment?

It will cool down.

Is the air cold or warm?

Can you sense the air entering your nostrils?

Pay attention to this air

We will now do deep breathing

You will inhale slowly through your nose to my count of 7

Hold it to the count of 7

Then exhale very slowly through your mouth to the count of 8

Maintain your focus on the breath

Don't let it wander away

It may get diverted to some random thoughts

Do not worry

Simply acknowledge the thought and bring your attention back to breathing

Take a slow and deep breath through your nose

1..

2...

3....

4.....

5....

6......

7......

Now gently hold this breath to the count of 7

1..

2...

3....

4.....

5....

6......

7......

Now exhale through your mouth slowly to the count of 8

1..

2...

3....

4.....

5....

6......

7......

8.......

Excellent!

Repeat once again

Take a slow and deep breath through your nose

1..

2...

3....

4.....

5....

6......

7......

Now gently hold this breath to the count of 7

1..

2...

3....

4.....

5....

6......

7......

Now exhale through your mouth slowly to the count of 8

1..

2...

3....

4.....

5....

6......

7......

8.......

Wonderful!!

Observe your breathing once again

Feel the calm in your breathing now

Take a deep breath

Feel the breath rising from your nostrils and diving deep inside your lungs

Follow its path as it travels to your solar plexus chakra

Feel the breath illuminating the whole solar plexus chakra from inside

Take a deep breath again

Feel your breath illuminating the solar plexus chakra once again

Feel the power this region holds

Think of the possibilities it holds

Visualize yourself living a successful life

Think of all the things you have always wanted to own

Feel them in your control

You have the ability to get anything you desire

The solar plexus chakra in your belly burns bright as a star

It gives you the potential to make anything possible

You just need to give a big push to anything you want

It is possible for you to do it once again

You have made that possible in the past

You can again make it possible very easily

You just need to think of it once

You simply need to make up your mind for it

You are ready to take any challenge in this world

You can face this world head-on

You are not afraid of challenges

They give you the motivation to work harder

Feel the energy building inside you

Imagine the strength you have

The power you can exercise

The influence you can wield

All this can help you on the way

You are capable of achieving anything

Feel the confidence inside you

Feel the power inside you

Feel the strength inside you

Remain in this position and just admire the moment

Let it fill you with vigor and vitality

Inhale

Exhale

Inhale

Exhale

Bring your awareness back to your breathing

Take a deep breath

Inhale

Exhale

Inhale

Exhale

Inhale

Exhale

Keeping your eyes closed observe your breathing closely

Keep your focus on your breathing

Inhale

Exhale

Inhale

Exhale

Bring your focus back to breathing

Feel your breath once again

Try to feel your surrounding

Try to feel your limbs without moving them

Relax

Sit for a few moments with your eyes closed

Now, you can open your eyes whenever you wish

Heart Chakra Healing

Lifestyle Changes for Heart Chakra Healing and Balancing

Start Paying Attention to Yourself

This chakra is always longing for love and care, but that necessarily doesn't have to come from others. We are always longing for love and attention but never care to show some love and attention to ourselves. If you are feeling low or depressed, treat yourself with a lavish dinner, a movie, a play, or anything else that sparks your interest. Don't let yourself starve for the love and attention of others.

Give Love Its Proper Space in Life

This chakra cannot function properly without love in life. Again this love can be for anything. If you are simply passionate about books, then also there is no problem as that would be enough to charge this chakra. However, you must find something to keep you engaged and your attention intact.

Get a Breather

Don't make yourself become an office rat. Give yourself some time to breathe. This chakra longs for something more than accolades and accomplishments. It wants relaxation and joy. If you are feeling very cramped up in the schedule, take out some time to treat yourself with something relaxing.

Try to Remain Motivated

Lack of motivation for anything can be a great turn down for this chakra. It is a chakra of enthusiasm about life. The energies at this level are intense, and that's why if you start remaining sorrowful and demotivated, this chakra can start losing its thrust.

Rekindle Your Relationship with Nature

If you are feeling low or dejected, try to go on a picnic somewhere close to nature and greenery. Plan a weekend in a forest or go hiking. Spending some time in the lap of nature can help in energizing this chakra.

Become More Accepting and Inviting

You must open yourself to new things, people, ideas, and experiences. Become more accepting in nature. Don't stick to specific things. Let the things of the past go away and accept new things in life. The same should be practiced in relationships as well as interests. The heart chakra requires you to be very open and accepting in nature. You must be ready to let the bygones be bygones and accept the present with open arms.

Learn New Art Forms

Learning new art forms can also ignite the energy in this chakra. This chakra has a strong creative spark, and learning new things can make that flame burn bright.

Green

The green color is good for this chakra. Living close to nature, eating green leafy vegetables, and wearing green clothes can help in restoring the energy balance in this chakra.

Yoga for Heart Chakra Healing and Balancing

- Eagle pose
- Camel pose
- Seated spinal twist
- Arm balances

Crystals for Heart Chakra Healing and Balancing

Green calcite, green kyanite, rose quartz, jade, emerald, and green tourmaline

Essential Oils for Heart Chakra Healing and Balancing

Rose, palmarosa, bergamot, geranium, ylang-ylang, neroli, lavender, and melissa

Heart Chakra Healing Meditation

Rep

Sit in a cross-legged posture

Close your eyes gently

Keep your spine upright

If you feel the need, you can use a backrest

Please maintain an upright posture throughout the meditation session

Keep your shoulders straight and equidistant

Your next should also remain straight

Please raise your chin a little upwards towards the sky

Just a little bit

You can place your hands in your lap or on your lap as you feel comfortable

During the course of the meditation, you will need to keep your eyes closed

You may get several thoughts related to your personal and professional thoughts during the meditation

Do not pay attention to them

Simply push them aside and pay attention to your breathing

Your focus should be on your awareness

This meditation session will help you in establishing a strong connection to your roots. It will help make you feel more grounded and firm. The feeling of contentment, self-sufficiency, and peace, which are missing, would become stronger in your heart after this session.

Sit calmly with your eyes gently closed

You don't need to think anything at this moment

This is the time to relax

If there are thoughts rushing to your mind, don't worry

Let them pass

They don't concern you at the moment

You are to become a calm and peaceful person at this moment

No need to think about anything

No need to focus on sorrow or happiness

No need to worry about failures and success

No need to worry about fears of pleasures

This is the moment to remain still and silent

You don't need to do anything

Bring your awareness on your breathing

Observe your breathing closely

Inhale

Exhale

Inhale

Exhale

Inhale

Exhale

Inhale

Exhale

Inhale

Exhale

Keep your focus glued to your breathing

Try to feel every aspect of your breathing

Is your breathing rapid at the moment?

It will cool down.

Is the air cold or warm?

Can you sense the air entering your nostrils?

Pay attention to this air

We will now do deep breathing

You will inhale slowly through your nose to my count of 7

Hold it to the count of 7

Then exhale very slowly through your mouth to the count of 8

Maintain your focus on the breath

Don't let it wander away

It may get diverted to some random thoughts

Do not worry

Simply acknowledge the thought and bring your attention back to breathing

Take a slow and deep breath through your nose

1..

2...

3....

4.....

5....

6......

7......

Now gently hold this breath to the count of 7

1..

2...

3....

4.....

5....

6……

7……

Now exhale through your mouth slowly to the count of 8

1..

2...

3....

4.....

5....

6……

7……

8…….

Excellent!

Repeat once again

Take a slow and deep breath through your nose

1..

2...

3....

4.....

5....

6......

7......

Now gently hold this breath to the count of 7

1..

2...

3....

4.....

5....

6......

7......

Now exhale through your mouth slowly to the count of 8

1..

2...

3....

4.....

5....

6......

7......

8.......

Wonderful!!

Observe your breathing once again

Feel the calm in your breathing now

Take a deep breath

Focus your awareness at the center of your chest

This is the point of the heart chakra

Try to visualize the green light coming out from this point

Look at your heart full of love and compassion

This heart has the power to heal many

It has pain for the whole world

It can forgive people

It can forget the things it can't forgive

It doesn't have space for hatred

It is just full of love and compassion

No one is capable of hurting such a heart

This heart can heal any kind of wound

It is full of calm and composure

There is no anxiety

There is no stress

There is no sorrow

There is no loneliness

There is just love and joy

Let all kind of pain, sorrow, misery, and bad memory evaporate

It is a part of life to have bad experiences

We have to learn to let go

We need to learn to move on

We need to learn to trust

We need to learn to love again

Take a deep breath once again

You are feeling light now

It feels as if a heavy load has got off your chest

It is time to rejoice

It is time to be happy

Enjoy this moment

Let it fill your heart and memory

Inhale

Exhale

Inhale

Exhale

Bring your awareness back to your breathing

Take a deep breath

Inhale

Exhale

Inhale

Exhale

Inhale

Exhale

Keeping your eyes closed observe your breathing closely

Keep your focus on your breathing

Inhale

Exhale

Inhale

Exhale

Bring your focus back to breathing

Feel your breath once again

Try to feel your surrounding

Try to feel your limbs without moving them

Relax

Sit for a few moments with your eyes closed

Now, you can open your eyes whenever you wish

Thorat Chakra Healing

Lifestyle Changes for Throat Chakra Healing and Balancing

Work On Improving Your Public Speaking Skills- Take Classes If Needed

Exposure to the public and the ability to express your thoughts clearly are two very important requirements of this chakra. They will remain suppressed if you keep running away from public speaking. The best way out is to develop public speaking skills. Speaking is as natural to people with a strong throat chakra as flying over the ocean is for seagulls. You don't need to teach a fish the art to swim. The hesitation can be there due to low energy in the throat center, but that can be easily rectified with the help of public speaking. If needed, you should take public speaking classes irrespective of the fact that public speaking is a part of your job description or not. Keeping this chakra unexplored can make your timid and ambiguous. You may also start facing problems in communicating even in close groups if the problem is ignored at this stage and you may not even be able to express yourself clearly.

Stop Lying

Some people simply become habitual liars without any specific reason. They don't lie for a cause but just to remain in practice. If you are among such people, you can be causing great harm to your throat chakra. This is the chakra of clear and concise speaking. If you start lying too much, the energies in this chakra may go down. You will start losing your convincing touch, and you may also start facing problems in conveying your message clearly to the masses.

Get Involved in Engaging Discussions

Take part in healthy discussions. The more you participate in healthy discussions, the more powerful this chakra will become. However, you must not convert the discussions to arguments as this chakra can easily become very dominating and egoistic. Simply focus on finding a conclusion to every discussion.

Practice Skygazing

Gazing at the clear blue sky can help in improving the energy levels in this chakra. It really likes the opportunity to feel connected to the vast, limitless expanse, and the clear blue sky provides it just that.

Blue

Blue color clothes and fruits are good for the development of this chakra.

Yoga for Throat Chakra Healing and Balancing

- Camel Pose
- Plow pose
- Bridge pose
- Triangle pose
- Warrior pose
- Extended side angle
- Shoulderstand

Crystals for Throat Chakra Healing and Balancing

Iolite, turquoise, lapis-lazuli, aquamarine, celestite,blue kyanite, and sodalite

Essential Oils for Throat Chakra Healing and Balancing

Rosemary, frankincense, lavender, and hyssop

Throat Chakra Healing Meditation

Sit in a cross-legged posture

Close your eyes gently

Keep your spine upright

If you feel the need, you can use a backrest

Please maintain an upright posture throughout the meditation session

Keep your shoulders straight and equidistant

Your next should also remain straight

Please raise your chin a little upwards towards the sky

Just a little bit

You can place your hands in your lap or on your lap as you feel comfortable

During the course of the meditation, you will need to keep your eyes closed

You may get several thoughts related to your personal and professional thoughts during the meditation

Do not pay attention to them

Simply push them aside and pay attention to your breathing

Your focus should be on your awareness

This meditation session will help you in finding your lost voice. There are times when we simply find it so hard to express ourselves. Saying even simple things become so difficult. Every word looks like a struggle. Then there are times when whatever you say means nothing to others. You find it virtually impossible to convey your message clearly and concisely. It happens with everyone. It is just a phase that comes in the lives of all of us. This meditation session will help you in regaining confidence in your voice and abilities.

Sit calmly with your eyes gently closed

You don't need to think anything at this moment

This is the time to relax

If there are thoughts rushing to your mind, don't worry

Let them pass

They don't concern you at the moment

You are to become a calm and peaceful person at this moment

No need to think about anything

No need to focus on sorrow or happiness

No need to worry about failures and success

No need to worry about fears of pleasures

This is the moment to remain still and silent

You don't need to do anything

Bring your awareness on your breathing

Observe your breathing closely

Inhale

Exhale

Inhale

Exhale

Inhale

Exhale

Inhale

Exhale

Inhale

Exhale

Keep your focus glued to your breathing

Try to feel every aspect of your breathing

Is your breathing rapid at the moment?

It will cool down.

Is the air cold or warm?

Can you sense the air entering your nostrils?

Pay attention to this air

We will now do deep breathing

You will inhale slowly through your nose to my count of 7

Hold it to the count of 7

Then exhale very slowly through your mouth to the count of 8

Maintain your focus on the breath

Don’t let it wander away

It may get diverted to some random thoughts

Do not worry

Simply acknowledge the thought and bring your attention back to breathing

Take a slow and deep breath through your nose

1..

2...

3....

4.....

5....

6......

7......

Now gently hold this breath to the count of 7

1..

2...

3....

4.....

5....

6......

7......

Now exhale through your mouth slowly to the count of 8

1..

2...

3....

4.....

5....

6......

7......

8.......

Excellent!

Repeat once again

Take a slow and deep breath through your nose

1..

2...

3....

4.....

5....

6......

7......

Now gently hold this breath to the count of 7

1..

2...

3....

4.....

5....

6......

7......

Now exhale through your mouth slowly to the count of 8

1..

2...

3....

4.....

5....

6......

7......

8.......

Wonderful!!

Observe your breathing once again

Feel the calm in your breathing now

Take a deep breath

Focus your awareness at the back of your throat

Through the eyes of your awareness try to visualize blue light coming from the back of the throat

Feel this light spreading to other parts of your body

Let it spread

Let it cover your shoulders

Let it go over to your head

Feel your whole body covered in this blue haze

This is the nourishing light of the throat chakra

It will make your communication stronger and clearer

Whatever you say, the world would listen

Just take a few deep breaths and let your mouth soak this blue light

Let it reach all the parts of the body

Just take deep breaths

Inhale

Exhale

Inhale

Exhale

Inhale

Exhale

Inhale

Exhale

Inhale

Exhale

Now imagine yourself speaking clearly and concisely

Visualize people listening to you with great attention

Look at their faces

They have the clarity

You are able to convey every word to them crystal clear

There is no ambiguity

There is no confusion

There is no hiding

You are now listening to them

It is such an important part of the process

It is so difficult to speak clearly without listening intently

Listen to the things they have to say

Absorb everything they want to tell

Now they will understand you clearly

Now you understand them clearly

There is no confusion now

There is no fear now

Breathe deeply

Inhale

Exhale

Inhale

Exhale

Inhale

Exhale

Bring your awareness back to your breathing

Take a deep breath

Inhale

Exhale

Inhale

Exhale

Inhale

Exhale

Keeping your eyes closed observe your breathing closely

Keep your focus on your breathing

Inhale

Exhale

Inhale

Exhale

Bring your focus back to breathing

Feel your breath once again

Try to feel your surrounding

Try to feel your limbs without moving them

Relax

Sit for a few moments with your eyes closed

Now, you can open your eyes whenever you wish

Third Eye Chakra Healing

Lifestyle Changes for Third Eye Chakra Healing and Balancing

Practice Brain Balancing Exercises

You will need to keep titillating your brain to give a good exercise to this chakra. Your cognitive abilities should be strong if you want to handle this chakra properly, and brain balancing exercises can help you in that. Give proper attention to your left and right brain and play games that challenge you intellectually.

Extend Your Level of Perception

This is a chakra of the unlimited power of perception. There can be no limit to the things this mind can imagine. However, like your imagination, your perception should also be wide. This is a skill that would have to be developed slowly with practice. Try to feel things around you. Try to feel the energies around you. Try to limit negative thoughts and think of all the positive things that could take place. The wider you take your power of perception, the easier it would become for you to handle the energies at this level.

Strengthen Your Root Chakra

One of the biggest problems at this chakra is fearfulness. This chakra can bring with itself unimaginable fears. Hallucination and paranoia grip people easily. If you are not grounded in reality properly, you can easily lose your balance and trip into a bottomless pit of fear and paranoia. Root chakra can help you in remaining grounded in reality. It also provides you a strong spiritual footing. You don't get easily swayed by imagination.To remain safe at this level, it is important to have a strong root chakra. The third eye chakra can also make you lose a sense of time and place. It dims the distinction of such things. The root chakra is also important for keeping you glued to the present time.

Stop Negative Thinking

Don't think about negative things. This chakra can multiply anything that you think several times over. So if there is the sweetness of emotion while working on this chakra, the things that may get multiplied will be positive, and hence, you'll have a positive experience. However, if you have negative things in your mind and they get caught in the handiwork of the third eye chakra, it can be a really scary experience for you. Even experience of energies in the surrounding environment can leave you really frightened. At this point, all that matters is the way you think and the manner in which you guide your perception.

Don't Have Negative Influences

Anything negative at this level should be avoided completely. You shouldn't even think about your enemies. Best, you shouldn't have enemies at all. Even if you have someone against whom you hold a grudge or think like an enemy, your mind can make that person stand against you in which you will be in a disadvantageous position. The game at the beginning is never fair at this level.

Stop Fantasizing and Daydreaming

Daydreaming and fantasizing should be discouraged as this chakra can give wings to fly to your dreams but may never allow it to land again. Try to stick to reality as much as possible. Do not let your attention wander around.

Indigo

Indigo is the color of this chakra. Wearing this color or keeping things of this color can help in keeping the third eye chakra active and energized.

Yoga for Third Eye Chakra Healing and Balancing

You would get benefits of yoga in this chakra, but there is no specific yoga for this chakra.

Crystals for Third Eye Chakra Healing and Balancing

Lepidolite, sugilite, lapis lazuli, amethyst, fluorite, tanzanite, clearquartz, star sapphire, and kyanite

Essential Oils for Third Eye Chakra Healing and Balancing

Frankincense, lavender, and sandalwood

Crown Chakra Healing

Lifestyle Changes for Crown Chakra Healing and Balancing

Be Thankful and Grateful

This chakra is the hardest to activate and achieve. There is no straight path to this chakra, and hence, you can only hope to find an indirect route. Being grateful and thankful lowers your burden of karma and makes you light. It is one of the ways that are advised in various religions to attain liberation. You must stick to that if you want to keep your karma low and path towards liberation clear. This attitude helps in keeping the conscience clear.

Get Involved in Charity of Any Type

There is nothing better than charity work to get the burden of karma off your chest. There is no need to donate all your money or home to charity but do as much as you can to help the people in need. Become more spiritual in nature. Try to find the good among the people you know. The more generous you are in your dealings, the easier it would become for you to clear the restrictions of karma.

Be Respectful of Elders

In the Hindu tradition, the blessings of the elders have great power. It believes that if you are respectful towards your elders and have work in good faith, you will get their blessings. These blessings can help you in maintaining the balance of energies in this chakra.

Yoga for Crown Chakra Healing and Balancing

- Headstand
- Shoulderstand

Crystals for Crown Chakra Healing and Balancing

Clear quartz, labradorite, moonstone, selenite, amethyst, and white topaz

Conclusion

Thank you for making it through to the end of this book, let's hope it was informative and able to provide you with all of the tools you need to achieve your goals whatever they may be.

The concept of chakras is amazing, and it provides great clarity over the things that happen in life, and we are not able to quite pinpoint the reasons for them.

This book has tried to explain the concept of chakras in detail and the ways in which it really affects our lives.

The emphasis of this book has been to explain that we may really not have any real control over the things that happen in life, but we can become proactive through the methods gives in this book and hold the command of our lives despite all the odds.

You can also get all the benefits of the process by following the simple steps given in the book.I hope that this book is really able to help you in achieving your goals.

Finally, if you found this book useful in any way, a review on Amazon is always appreciated!

Reiki Healing for Beginners:

The Ultimate Guide to Meditation and Healing to Increase Your Energy and Defeat the Daily Anxiety

Introduction

Congratulations onpurchasing*Reiki Healing for Beginners: The Ultimate Guide to Reiki Meditation and Reiki Healing to Increase Your Energy and Defeat the Daily Anxiety*, and thank you for doing so.

Just by purchasing this book, you have already taken a big step to learning all about Reiki and how to heal yourself and others. This book will act as a great guide to help you master the art of Reiki healing and be able to heal yourself, animals, plants, others even if they aren't physically present with you.

The following chapters will discuss everything you need to know about Reiki; it will prepare you for your first attunement and how to self-attune yourself. This book will teach you how to heal your body and mind and getting rid of anxiety and negative emotions which influences the health of the body. You will also learn how to open each chakra with Reiki, perform self-healing on yourself, master distance healing, and how to send Reiki to a specific event because when it comes to Reiki, time and distance do not matter! Healing the body, mind, and spirit has never been easier, good luck on your journey!

There are plenty of books on this subject on the market, thanks again for choosing this one! Every effort was made to ensure it is full of as much useful information as possible; please enjoy!

Chapter 1: What Is Reiki

Reiki is a very powerful healing energy than can be used to heal the body, mind, and soul. It was discovered by no one other than Mikao Usui, who was a Buddhist monk who was able to understand this energy and channel it in order to heal himself and others around him. Usui was born into a wealthy family in 1865; he had access to a well-rounded education and chose to study psychology, theology, and medicine. Through his years of learning and training in the monastery, he eventually decided to start his own training, taking place in a cave of Mount Kurama. For 21 days, he meditated, fasted, and prayed continuously and on the 21st day, in his vision, he saw Sanskrit symbols which helped him develop his own system of healing. He names this system 'The Usui Treatment Method for Body and Mind,' or what is currently known as Reiki.

The word 'Reiki' is made out of two Japanese words, 'Rei' and 'Ki.' If we were to translate these words into English, then the meaning will be rather twisted since an exact spiritual translation is rather difficult. 'Rei' is defined as a ghost while 'Ki' is defined as vapor, these definitions only point in the direction of what we are looking for, but it is not the whole picture.

In a spiritual context, 'Rei' is interpreted as the Universe or also known as the Higher Intelligence, which guides every living thing, spirit, and functions the universe. Rei can also be defined as subtle wisdom which permeates everything the living and the dead. This wisdom guides the development of life, the creation, evolution, and the unfolding of many galaxies. This power is really extraordinary and big, but if you look at it more on a human level, this energy acts as a source of guidance which will help us any time we require assistance in life. This infinite nature is constantly around us and it is always available to help us. It is also called 'God' in many cultures and religions, but either way, this nature is all-knowing.

'Ki,' on the other hand, is a non-physical energy that inspires, animates, and encourages everything that is living. This energy is everywhere, in humans, animals, and even plants. Those who have a high Ki are confident and strong; they are able to take on whatever life throws at them with no doubts. But when this energy is low, their strength is replaced with weakness and may even get sick. Ki is also known as the life force, odic force, bioplasma, and orgone by many religions and cultures. This so-called life force leaves when the body when it dies. Although it is unknown what happens after death, many religions believe that the soul or life force moves on by reincarnating, going to heaven, or going to Summerland which is the spiritual world on the other side. Either way, this energy still lives on.

Combining the two words, Reiki can be described as the non-physical healing energy that guides your life force by the Higher Intelligence, also known as God or Deity. Many refer to it as spiritual guidance and spiritual healing for your body, mind, and soul. However, this is only a technical definition; Reiki itself is so much more. Many of those who practice Reiki and the Reiki healing practice agree that this energy or force has an intelligence of its own; it is able to understand what one needs and where this healing is required. Reiki cannot be controlled, which is why it is not limited by the ability and experience of those who practice Reiki.

As we had mentioned earlier, Reiki is a power. This power liaises and activates the central healer. The central healer, in this case, is that inner part of you which has the record of what exactly needs to be done for you to be well. Reiki is lead by the spirit and therefore, it forms its basis on love with Godly aptitude that is ever humble and very beneficial. The purpose of Reiki is to mend and bring together every power system in our bodies.

The power systems are mental, emotional, spiritual as well as the physical organizations of our bodies. It digs deep into a specific attribute that is in need of healing at the time of its initiation. Therefore the root of the problem could reside in any of the mentioned systems of the body. There are examples of asthma and allergy.

These conditions are mainly brought about as a result of unregulated emotions. Whenever you are exposed to any medical curative procedure, it is not automatic that the procedure will lead make you heal. Instead, they are the systems that will team up to agree that the root of the problem has been eliminated.

Many are times where medical attention alone has failed to yield to the permanent healing of an ailing person. That is where Reiki comes in. You are left feeling relaxed and peaceful, able to take up life at large. It is the prime role of your central healer to obtain results more directly and in an ideal mode; therefore, Reiki kindles as well as enhances the inner healer.

How Reiki Works

When the power of life flows through us, we are kept alive. We also refer this to as life-force. There are passages for this force within our bodies, namely: nadis, chakras, and meridians. The movement within our bodies also takes place in an energy zone referred to as the aura.

It helps to maintain the body organs as well as body cells, enabling them to work well. The flow must be free from any form of interference; otherwise, it will lead to a breakdown in either one or many tissues and body organs within the physical body. In other words, the force reacts to our feelings and thoughts. The flow feels disturbed every time we agree with the negativities in our feelings or thoughts concerning our bodies.

These negative thoughts will later join with the power field, thus, leading to a breakdown in the smooth running of life force. In the end, this will lead to a general breakdown of the normal functioning of the body and its organs. It is at this stage that Reiki finds a basis for operation. It heals by running through the energy field that is mostly affected by pumping-in the right energy.

It goes deeper to find where the negative thoughts are being harbored; then, it creates the level of positive energies around them. The harmful energy is replaced by the right and helpful energy. Therefore Reiki will clean, make straight, and then heal the pathways. This, in turn, leads to a smooth flowing of life-force in a natural and healthy way.

Reiki Levels

Reiki has got levels in which it operates in. They are often referred to as degrees. We will take a look at three major levels basically; level 1 or first degree, level two or second degree and lastly, level three or third degree.

Reiki Level 1: The First Degree

The first level is known as a 'beginner' level; it is open to anyone. Everyone and anyone has the power to perform Reiki on themselves. The goal of this level is to open the energy channels, where Ki flows. It permits the student to channel the Reiki energy on a physical level with the use of only one initiation, the Usui Tibetan system which will be covered in the following chapters. After this initiation, the student will start to feel the energy flowing into and through their hands which can be perceived as tingling, heat, buzzing, coolness, or any other sensations within your hands or throughout your body. For some people, those sensations within the hands or body sometimes don't happen straight away, but rather sometime after the initiation has been performed.

When the energy is released, it harmonizes and balances the seven main chakras, which are the major energy centers located and spread throughout the top of the head, down the spine, and to the bottom where the tailbone resides. This level is open to anyone with or without experience; the teaching of this method often takes one weekend to teach. However, this connection can never be undone; it is permanent and can be used whenever the student wishes.

The amount of this energy that has been channeled after the initiation varies differently, but when Reiki is used more and more, that energy becomes more constant. The energy on the physical level consists of 80% to 90%, with the other being located within the emotional, mental, and spiritual levels.

Reiki Level 2: The Second Degree

Before moving on to the Second Degree, the student must first complete the First Degree. It usually takes around twenty-one days and up to three months to practice and perfect the First Degree, with regular self-treatments and practices throughout the weeks. In the Second Degree, the central channels have been expanded and opened to a greater level with an increase in the channeled energy. This is also where the Reiki healing is expanded and practiced on others. With that in mind, the student also receives three Reiki symbols, the Power Symbol, the Distance Symbol, and the Mental/Emotional Symbol, which will be discussed in the following chapters. Reiki symbols are used to draw the qualities and energy of those symbols in order to connect more deeply to the universe and succeed in the Reiki energy channel.

Due to the attunement process and intensity of the Second Degree, there has to be at least twenty-one to a full three months passing period on the level one Reiki before moving on to the next level. There is usually one attunement required in the second degree with the focus on the heart chakra and opening the central channel.

Reiki Level 3: The Third Degree

This level increases the student's capacity once again. The student also receives the Usui Master Symbol, which will help him make contact with his own inner truth and work on a more spiritual level. This level is also known as Inner Master because it enables practitioners to recognize that everyone is a master of their own path, destiny, and each person is responsible for their own life. The Third Degree also help the student find it's life path and the required changes in order to live the life that the student wants.

Reiki Level 4: Reiki Master

The Reiki Master is considered to be a teacher of Reiki, with a lot of energy and knowledge to be able to teach new Reiki practitioners and attune them to Reiki at the beginning of their journey. There is also a Reiki Master attunement that needs to be received with its corresponding symbol in order to feel confident and comfortable when it comes to attuning others. The one who chooses to follow this level will also learn a variety of techniques in order to be able to attune and initiate others. Reaching this level also demonstrates a deep commitment to the Reiki practice with the knowledge and skills to be able to perform and teach others of Reiki healing and self-discovery.

Ethical Considerations as You Use Reiki

1. Reiki in itself is not a curative but rather preventive remedy that does not need to eliminate or take up the place of any medical directives. When using reiki, it is advisable to continue with the medications if, by the time you began reiki, you were on any form of medication. Reiki comes in to complement but not substitute any other form of therapy. Again, there is no point in carrying forward any prescribed medication in exchange with reiki.

2. Reiki is an exercise that requires that one has to be well qualified in order to realize maximum benefit from it. Therefore, it is very important that you research the reiki practitioner who will handle your situation. Make sure you get to know his background, his expertise, and at least know his past record in that field.

3. As you continue with the procedure, you need to understand that reiki is still being researched on, and any future changes or improvements are expected. You also need to know that reiki is not a scientific study but rather a spiritual exercise.

4. Before you get into the Reiki game, it's advisable that you take time and share with the teacher or the practitioner about your previous methods of healing you have been using. It is very important to do so in order to avoid the use of excessive health remedies, which may turn out to be overwhelming or even non-productive.

5. You need to have faith in reiki. Faith only will make your problem solvable even before the stipulated period elapses. The fact that Reiki is a spiritual exercise; faith contributes to a greater percentage of your healing in the process.

Chapter 2: Basics of Reiki

Anyone can learn Reiki and access its energy since it doesn't depend on any ability or talent of the practitioner. The Reiki attunement is one of the most powerful spiritual experiences, and without it, you can't heal yourself with Reiki. This attunement process is guided by a God-like consciousness, also known as Rei, it sees into the practitioner's body and understands what needs to be cleansed, healed, and unblocked. Often, this practice is guided by spiritual beings who aid and implement the process; this is why many of those who underwent the attunement report experiencing healings, visions, and even personal messages.

The attunement is such a powerful energy that it can even increase your psychic sensitivity, such as the opening of the third eye, developing psychic abilities, and increasing intuitive awareness. Once the Reiki attunement has been completed, Reiki will be within you for the rest of your life. Whenever you need healing, it will be there, you can never lose touch with it, and it does not wear off. You only require one attunement when first accessing this energy and one attunement throughout each of the Reiki levels, but many practitioners choose to carry on more than one due to its many benefits such as adding an extra value of this level, strength, and power into the healing. The channeling of that energy becomes easier as well as an increase in clarity of mind, raised vibrations, a higher level of consciousness, healing within the body or any personal problems, and an increase in psychic sensitivity.

It is required that you achieve the attunement because, without it, you will not have access to its healing energies. This process can also connect you to your Higher Self to discover your purpose and meaning of life, which is what a spiritual journey is all about.

The best way to get access to the Reiki energy and get a Reiki attunement is by seeking a Reiki Master. Since Reiki is such powerful healing energy, it is recommended by many that it is done physically, not through video calls, videos, or DVDs. Although distance attunement can sometimes work, it is not guaranteed that you will receive all the energy, a part of the attunement requires for the Reiki Master to touch certain parts of the body like hands, neck, head, and some other parts. This physical contact is important for it transmits and enables the student to use Reiki.

But there is always another way, just like Mikao Usui, who didn't have a master and was able to attune himself through a twenty-one-day process of meditation and fasting. Seeking a Reiki Master to attune you to this energy and teach you Reiki healing is done within eight to twelve hours, which is a faster method. However, following a self-attunement is all about one's self-discovery. The attunement process is all about raising the student's energy level so high that you are able to reconnect with your Higher Self and the universal energy. Throughout this process, your vibrations and frequency rise drastically and you receive insight into the world around you. However, the self-attunement process does not give one a certificate of completion of the level one Reiki like sessions with Reiki Masters does.

Because of the life force flowing in us, through chakras, nadis, and meridians, we are able to support our body functions. However, this energy can also become corrupted, causing a failure in supporting organs and cells within the body. Since this energy is so pure, negative thoughts and feelings directed at us or certain parts of our bodies, either unconsciously or consciously, can affect the body. The goal of the twenty-one-day process of self-attuning yourself is to train your mind to be able to block, stop these negative thoughts with meditation and be able to open the palm, heart, and crown chakras.

Since Reiki is a very pure form of energy, you have to start cleansing your body, mind, and soul at least one week before your attuning appointment if you choose to get a Reiki Master or throughout the twenty-one-day journey of self-attunement. The preparation process below can also be used for those who are planning on getting a Reiki Master to attune them to the universal healing energy, except fitted into a one-week span process.

The preparation process is just as important as the attunement, it will allow the energies to work more effectively, on a faster pace, and they will provide more benefits for the body, mind, and soul. Cleansing beforehand is how you achieve the perfect state and become a vessel for such a powerful energy. Many instructors and Reiki Masters will provide you certain special care instructions, but if they don't, then don't worry, this guide will tell you everything you need to do prior to your Reiki attunement, whether it is a physical attunement or a self attunement!

1) Eat healthily

The point of preparing before your attunement is to purify your body so you will become closer to the same vibration and level that your Higher Self is. Not only eating healthy can cleanse the body of toxins, but it can also keep the body healthy! Stay clear of foods such as fish, fowl, and meat, for they are often filled with female hormones, toxins, pesticides, and penicillin. Do not eat any chocolate or sweets even though it is tempting, but your body and Higher Self will thank you for it later! You can even choose to fast for a couple of hours a day, but that choice should be made by you.

2) Drink healthily

Mikao Usui spent twenty-one days fasting, but that doesn't mean you don't have to. Consider doing a juice or water fast for a couple of days; you don't have to carry it on for a whole week or twenty-one days if you don't want to. The choice is yours to make, let your intuition guide you. Do not drink drinks that possess caffeine; they create an imbalance within the endocrine and nervous systems. Also, refrain from drinking any alcohol.

3) Medication

If you are on any prescribed medication, then do not stop taking it.

4) No smoking

Stop smoking for the time being. Not only is smoking bad for the lungs, but it is also a negative form of energy. Consider giving it up, but for the time being and refrain yourself from smoking. You need to maintain a pure body in order to be able to channel the energy that you will receive in your attunement process.

5) Meditation

Spend at least one hour a day meditating with any techniques that you like. Through meditation, you are able to cleanse your mind and release any fear, doubt, anxiety, anger, hate, worry, and jealousy. There are countless benefits of meditation, but most importantly, it is able to create a sacred space within your body. When meditating to achieve self-attunement, spend a week each meditating on opening and cleaning your three chakras which are used in Reiki, the heart, the palm, and the crown chakra.

6) No electronics

Try to eliminate the use of electronics, especially TV, computers, and the radio. Also, avoid reading the newspapers.

7) Be alone

Spend some time alone; we often pick up other peoples vibrational energy and many times that energy is far from positive. Spend some quality time alone, taking care of yourself and your body. Do something that you love to raise your vibrations.

8) Exercise

Another method for relieving the body of negativity and toxins is through exercise. Consider going hiking in nature, biking, or swimming. If you don't have access to any of those, a simple jog for a couple of minutes a day can do wonders!

9) Nature

Spend some time in Nature, go to the beach, a park, or go hiking.

10) Cleanse your house

Using sage or any other incense, cleanse your house and sacred space to get rid of any previous negative energy, impurities, and to lighten up the mood. Cleaning your house is another way of cleansing and purifying it.

11) Self-love

Love is one of the purest forms of energy, and those who possess a lot of self-love for themselves have very high vibrations. Practice self-love and self-acceptance. You are you for a reason, you were born for a reason, and you were born to receive and give love to your family, friends, or partner. Accept yourself for who you are and learn to cherish yourself.

12) No stress

Minimize your task or work intake. If possible, then take some time off or wait until it's the holiday season to get attuned to Reiki so you can relax and not stress about your responsibilities.

13) Cleanse your aura

Do a cleansing ritual of your aura. There are many methods of cleansing involving incense, crystals, or simply visualization, so take some time to cleanse your aura.

14) Sleep

Get at least eight hours of sleep to give the body energy and strength for its self-discovery journey.

15) Pray

Pray to the Higher Beings for a successful attunement and guidance throughout the process.

One Day or Few Hours Prior Your Attunement

1) Reflect

Sit down and reflect on everything that you have done to prepare for this moment. Think about how your thoughts, emotions, or any physical sensations have changed from before you started preparing for Reiki. Take some time to relax, reflect, and listen to your intuition. This is a perfect time to set an intention of successfully self-attune yourself.

2) Deep breathes

Deep breathing can help calm your body if you are nervous and tend to anything that you feel you must do before the process.

3) Wash yourself

Take a relaxing bath or a shower to help you relax furthermore. It is also helpful if you either sprinkle a handful of salt into the water of your bath for cleansing of negativity or tie some salt up in a cloth and use it to wash your body.

4) Eat and drink

Make sure you will not be distracted by hunger or thirst throughout your session. A few hours before, make sure you drink plenty of water and have a healthy breakfast. Do not drink a lot of water right before your attunement. You don't want to feel distracted by the need to use the bathroom.

5) Comfort is key

Wear something that is light, not tight, to provide you the best comfort.

Say you've done all those things, you've meditated for twenty-one days straight, cleansed your body, and managed to open the three chakra points, so what do you do now?

On the twenty-first day, set a time for yourself when precisely you want to begin your self-attunement, specifically after you've done everything that was listed above. Turn off any electronic devices, lock your doors, or ask your family or whoever you live with to not to disturb you until you are done. Proceed by sitting down with your legs crossed and your spine, nice, tall, and straight. Place your hands on your knees with the palms facing up, making a mudra hand position which is similar to an okay-hand-gesture.

Close your eyes and start to breathe deeply. Inhale through your nose, hold the breath for three seconds and exhale through your mouth, holding it out for three seconds. Repeat for a few minutes; you are relaxing your body and preparing your mind to receive the attunement. Make sure no thoughts disturb you and set the intention of banishing any negativity that is left through the exhale of your breath. With every exhale, your body becomes purer and raises its vibrations, getting ready to take on Reiki. Once you feel that you are ready to move on to the next step, continue to breathe deeply and say the words below with a strong and clear voice:

'I call upon the energy of the Universe, to grant me access to Reiki 1, and to be able to heal myself, and others with practice. I ask this power to permit me to channel its energy and grant me its knowledge and sight of the universe around me.'

Set an intention for receiving Reiki 1 attunement, and for becoming the vessel for such energy. Have only good intentions for its use, sit in quiet with only deep breathing for a minute or two before continuing. Visualize a bright white light emerging from above you, the light of the Universe as it comes down upon you through your crown chakra, at the top of your head. Keep on repeating the intention of receiving Reiki as the energy and light shines down upon you and enters through your mind. It travels down your spine, clearing and unblocking all the existing chakras within your body. Feel your spirits lift up, and your vibrational energy heighten. You might start to feel tingling sensations through the top of your head and on other parts of your body.

Focus on that energy and direct it all to the top of your head. Take some time to imagine that energy opening up and activating the crown chakra, let yourself feel the warmth or tingling sensations at the top of your head.

Move your focus to your heart chakra, let that energy travel down and surround your heart. Let yourself feel the emotions of self-love and blessing fill your body; those are the highest of vibrations. Thank the universe for letting you channel Reiki and for this great opportunity to be able to learn to heal yourself and others around you.

Now direct your attention to the palm of your hands; this is where all the healing and magic will happen. Visualize the white light emerging from your hands, channeling the universal energy and healing. Let the universe give you blessings and energy to be able to access Reiki.

Continue thinking and setting your intentions for channeling Reiki; let your frequency and vibrations raise. Bring your attention to your Higher Self, call out to them and ask for assistance, build a connection to be able to channel Reiki. Enjoy the feeling throughout your body, negativity fading into nothing, tingling sensation all over your body. Do not rush, take as long as you need to achieve the Reiki attunement.

After the Attunement Process

1) Don't panic

If you can't feel the energy straight away then don't panic, it's completely normal. Many times the attunement process takes effect after the session is over, which is why when you have attuned yourself or a Reiki Master has attuned you, find a comfortable, quiet, and relaxing spot with no distractions. You may want to meditate, take a nap, or lie down after the session.

2) Drink water

After doing any energy work, you should drink at least one to two glasses of water to recover your energy and avoid being thirsty.

3) Eat

You will start to feel hungry or thirsty, sometimes even right after your attunement. Eating is a way to ground the body, make sure to eat a healthy meal or snack if you feel necessary.

4) Reflect

Think about how the attunement made you feel. Did you feel any heat, tingling sensations, or see any visions? Write everything down; it will help you draw upon the energy in the future when you are practicing healing yourself. Do an activity that can help connect to what just happened to you, listen to calming music and think back to what just happened. It is suggested that you meditate for a few minutes before continuing with your day.

Many of those who have experienced the attunement claimed to feel nothing, and that is because their bodies are already on the same level and frequency of the required one, making you only feel certain tingling sensations or warmth. Those practitioners who started off on very low and negative vibrations feel their bodies and the energy actually circle within them during the attunement.

One should always be ready for any side effects that will occur after the very first Reiki attunement process. This is because, through the attunement, you were being exposed to a completely different frequency, vibration, and energy which changes the way you feel emotionally and physically. There are many side effects that you should be aware of such as chest pain, runny nose, headaches, blurred vision, heavy limbs, diarrhea, cranial pressure, and some others which will make you feel 'out of the ordinary.' This is the way for your body to release hidden toxins. If that does occur, then make sure you drink plenty of water and lie down and rest your body.

There are emotional effects too. Many feel certain emotions that they haven't felt in a long time, especially sadness or anger. Past emotional traumas can re-surface. These negative emotions or past feelings are here because you haven't fully let go of them yet, but now is the chance. Cry it all out, or yell it away, this opportunity acts as a final push of those negative feelings out of your body, releasing you from their grasp forever. Reiki heals you not just physically but emotionally too.

There are many spiritual effects that come out after the Reiki attunement. Because of the new energy that has been introduced to you, your senses become heightened, and your third eye opens. Not only can you receive messages, visions, new knowledge, or insights but you can also begin to doubt your own beliefs, religion, and your view on spirituality. This may be due to your sense of identity but do not let it bother you. Spend some time exploring your new psychic gifts, spend time in nature, or meditate. Any spiritual answers that you might have will eventually show themselves to you; all you have to do is be patient.

After the attunement process, the practitioner is able to do Reiki and practice Reiki healing on themselves. But there are still tips you should know before jumping into a Reiki healing, and these tips are called 'the three pillars of Reiki.'

Mikao Usui, the founder of Reiki, opened his knowledge decided to teach his students Reiki, within those studies, he introduces the three pillars of Reiki which are practices that are all suggested when performing a Reiki healing. These practices are able to put the practitioner into a centered and calm state of mind, allows more intuitive information and work to flow, and it creates mindfulness. These are all necessary to make sure the Reiki healing works and process flows by more smoothly.

Gassho

The first pillar of Reiki is Gassho, which corresponds with centering, breathing, meditation, and asking to channel the Reiki energy. This is all about getting into the right mindset of healing and receiving the flow of Reiki energy. Setting intentions and breathing properly is how you prepare for the Reiki healing session. The word 'Gassho' means two hands coming together; it is the 'prayer' hand position that represents gratitude, balance, respect, and focus.

During meditation, this hand position helps to focus, quiet, and clear the mind, which is necessary for a Reiki energy healing. It shows gratitude to the universe for granting the practitioner Reiki.

In a seated position with your legs crossed, bring your hands together in a prayer position. Close your eyes, take a deep breath, and bring your awareness to the top of the hand, where the middle fingers touch. Clear your mind of any thoughts and set an intention of gratitude and focus throughout this quick meditation. If you find your mind wandering away, press the two middle fingers together to gain back your focus. Meditate for at least fifteen to thirty minutes daily or a couple of days prior to performing a Reiki healing session.

Reji-ho

The second pillar is called Reiji-ho where 'Reji' means the indication of Reiki power, while 'ho' means methods. In this case, you are asking for the guidance of receiving and channeling the Reiki energy. This practice helps receive Reiki in a specific place, where the energy is most needed. You are switching the 'on' button for the energy, remember after your first attunement, you already have the energy within you, and all you have to do is turn it on. Place your intention where you wish to direct the Reiki to and ask for assistance.

Begin by raising your hands, forming the Gassho position, which is the 'prayer' hand position and center it in front of your heart. Close your eyes and call out to the Reiki energy to flow through you. Then, move your hands and center them directly above your third eye, still in the 'prayer' position. Ask to be guided to where Reiki healing is needed the most. Let your hands move by themselves, leading to where the Reiki energy is needed. Keep your mind clear and don't think about the outcome of the Reiki energy, trust this process to heal you wherever you need healing.

Chiryo

The third and last pillar is called chiryo which means the treatment. This one is used when you give Reiki to your client or whoever you are trying to heal. In this case, both the client and the practitioner experience guidance and healing from the treatment. The practitioner begins by placing their own hand over the client's crown chakra, not touching but hovering above in the air. Both of the people involved breath deeply and ask for guidance and healing. The hand of the practitioner will move to where there is a pull or where their intuition tells them to.

Reiki Tools

Reiki Treatment is a holistic alternative treatment practice that involves the use of various tools and resources. Reiki Tools are meant to facilitate the process as well as ensuring that the client or yourself is kept as comfortable as possible throughout the treatment process. Furthermore, some of the tools and resources are also meant to facilitate the creation of the most ideal environment for a typical Reiki treatment. This is because; Reiki treatment is a fairly delicate process that should be handled by uttermost care. This section will discuss one of the common Reiki tools and related resources. Keep in mind that these tools are preferred but not required. Reiki is a practice that can also be done in the comfort of your home and your own mind.

Massage Table

Perhaps the most vital tool that must be present in each and every Reiki treatment room is the massage table. The Massage Table is the area where the client or yourself will lie throughout the Reiki Treatment session. Due to the fact that the amount of time that a client is expected on the table can be quite long, it is important to take several measures in order to ensure that the table is ideal for the treatment. First and foremost, the table should be as comfortable as possible. In light of this fact, you should consider using extra padding for the top surface to maximize the client or yourself comfort. Secondly, the table should also have strong support to accommodate clients or your own of different weights and sizes. Finally, the color of the table should be bright enough and one that resonates with the overall setting of the room.

However, if you are studying Reiki to heal yourself and/or your friends or family, you can always use the couch, the floor, or the bed for your practices. If it will become something continuous, make sure that you pick a sacred spot within your house that will continue to be used for your reiki practices. That way, the Reiki energy will always be floating within the room.

Reiki Pendulum

A special pendulum should be used in conducting the Reiki treatment process. The pendulum can be used as a diagnostic tool when analyzing the energy levels in the body. The Reiki pendulum must be infused with universal healing energy so as to make it an appropriate device for treatment. A typical Reiki Pendulum can consist of a charged crystal suspended by a string that is equally charged.

Reiki Symbol Stones

Reiki Symbol Stones are special stones that are used in the Reiki treatment process. The stones contain several images that are the cornerstone of Reiki treatment and healing. There is a stone for the Master Symbol, one for the Power Symbol, Harmony Symbol, and finally, a stone containing the Completion Symbol. The Reiki Symbol Stones can be used at various points during the treatment session with the aim of ensuring that there is maximum energy channeled to the client or yourself while at the same time, establishing the appropriate connection with external forces.

Reiki Treatment Cards

Just as is the case with the stones, Reiki treatment can also be enhanced with the use of special cards with each and every card having a specific role in the process. For instance, the set of cards contains one that is designated as the listening card. This card is meant to enable the client or yourself to listen to their own internal rhythm and connect with a force higher than them. Similarly, there is another card referred to as the *Freshen up Card*. The second card is vital in facilitating body purification making it easy for the client or yourself to rejuvenate and regain lost energy.

Timer or Stop Watch

Reiki is a rather precise practice that involves subjecting the client or yourself to different types of treatment meant to handle specific ailments that the person is having. Each and every treatment is precisely timed, and thus, it is important to know when to switch from one treatment position to another. For instance, the first position treatment that involves cupping the client's or your own face with your arms must take place for a specific period before switching to the second position which is the sides of the head. A timer or stopwatch can be set for each treatment position so as to ensure that the practitioner is able to spend adequate time on each treatment. The timer will, therefore, enhance the overall effectiveness of the treatment.

Reiki Energy Pendant

The Reiki Energy Pendant is essential in enabling the practitioner to invoke the much-needed Universal Life Force that is the basis of any form of Reiki treatment. The Pendant is worn by the Reiki Practitioner as a symbol of power and energy.

Reiki Symbol Poster

Despite the emphasis on bright colors, it is important to ensure that the treatment room is not an entirely dull affair. You should have some appropriate fittings and even literature that help your clients or yourself connect with the treatment. The Reiki Treatment Poster is perhaps one of the most commonly used tools or resources to make the Room appealing to the client or yourself. It is basically a poster that can be placed on the wall and it contains the images of several Reiki Symbols. You can get a good artist to make you a nice poster with unique bright colors that will improve the overall aesthetics of the treatment room.

Reiki CD

Having some audio material playing on a CD player is also very important during the treatment session. The audio CD contains a lot of information that can enlighten and empower the client or yourself throughout the treatment process. The Reiki Treatment CD is even more effective than the literature material such as Magazines since the client or yourself can listen to it at all times, even while concentrating on something else. All in all, there are several tools that must be used in each and every Reiki treatment session. The overall effectiveness of any treatment session will depend largely on the availability of all these tools that each play a unique role in ensuring the entire treatment process is indeed a success. You can also consider putting on some soft and light melody in the background to help you focus more.

Using Crystals for Reiki Treatment

Treatment and Healing by Reiki can be made more effective by using various tools. Crystals are among the most commonly used Reiki Treatment tools. There are several benefits associated with the use of crystals for Reiki treatment, including its ability to facilitate energy balancing as well as speeding up the healing process.

Some practitioners usually shy away from crystals on account of the amount of information that one should have before commencing the process. This is because, before you can start using crystals for Reiki healing, you must know which stone to place at different chakras. It can be quite confusing at first but once you wrap your head around the color-coding system, then you will realize the immense benefits that come about with crystals as a way of enhancing the Reiki treatment process.

Animal Reiki

Reiki can also be administered to animals with some of the effects on animals being similar to the effects on human beings. The overall goal of animal treatment is to make the animal feel comfortable, calm and stress free. Animals are very unique in terms of their behavior and temperament. Animals usually experience various situations that can result to stress, trauma and even withdrawal on the part of the animal.

Animal Reiki usually takes the form of meditation that seeks to connect the practitioner with the animal through the universal life force. It might not be easy to get the animal to settle down and calm down for Reiki treatment. However, if you know what to do in order to attract the attention of the animal, then you can calm it down and commence the meditation process.

Sometimes, animal meditation might involve the use of touch. However, at times touch might not be required when it comes to animal treatment, and meditation alone might do the trick. Meditation can take the form of staring into the eyes of the animal for a considerable amount of time. The objective is to create an emotional connection with the animal and harness its negative energy while at the same time, projecting your positive energy into the animal. The positive energy that you channel to the animal during the mediation process can ensure that the animal is able to recover from any stress and trauma. The positive energy can also facilitate physical healing on the part of the animal.

Clears Imbalance

Reiki treatment also clears imbalance on the part of the animal. When there is an imbalance in the body of an animal or even a human being for that matter, it is easy for them to contact diseases and become unhealthy. Reiki treatment in animals seeks to create a harmonious balance of energy flow within the animal's body. The balanced flow of energy makes the animal much healthier and in addition to improving its overall wellness.

One of the reasons why many animals might need Reiki Treatment is because of past trauma. Animals are at times mistreated or they might get injured while doing something. The overall trauma can result to a sustained state of fear on the part of the animal and this is not good at all. The Reiki treatment seeks to create a calm environment that reassures the animal that there is indeed nothing to fear.

Relieve Symptoms and Pain

Animals are naturally very active creatures. This implies that no matter what you do, your animal is bound to get into some sort of injury or the other. The animal will, therefore, be in pain, and even though you can administer pain killer medication, Reiki treatment can also be used as a natural remedy for pain. The treatment will not necessarily eliminate the pain, but it will certainly reduce the same.

Reduces Side Effects of Drugs

Some of the drugs administered to the animals might have adverse side effects. Such side effects might include nausea, pain, and anxiety, among others. To this end, Reiki treatment can be used in the treatment of side effects associated with drugs. The animal will thus end up being much more comfortable even while being subjected to conventional medication.

A Non-Invasive Form of Healing the Animal

While physical contact is very important in human Reiki treatment, the same is not a must when it comes to Reiki treatment for animals. Because of this fact, Reiki treatment for animals is regarded to be a non-invasive treatment that can provide healing without interfering too much with the animal. This makes it convenient to both the person offering the treatment and animal that is being subjected to the treatment.

Effective as a Form of Palliative Care

At times, animals, just like human beings, might suffer from terminal illnesses. While such diseases can cause a lot of pain and distress to the animal, a well designed palliative care program can ensure that the pain and distress is significantly addressed. Reiki Treatment for animals can go a long way in improving the overall quality of care offered to terminally ill animals. The treatment will make the animal feel as comfortable as possible, reduce pain, and eliminate stress and anxiety.

Used in Diagnosis

Treatment with Reiki can be used as diagnosis for further condition. This is because the practitioner is able to effectively communicate with the animal, and this communication can reveal pain and other underlying conditions that the animal might be suffering from. Reiki can, therefore, offer insightful information that can be used by the animal owner to initiate further treatment practices.

Distance Reiki Treatment for Animals

As earlier noted, Reiki treatment for animals does not necessarily require physical contact. The animal can be treated by simply channeling positive healing energy from the universal life force. It is, therefore, possible to treat animals that are far away from the practitioner. This is ideal for large animals that cannot be easily transported to a Reiki treatment clinic. Similarly, the long distance treatment option can also be applied to animals that are wild and considered dangerous to be in close contact with the practitioner.

When an Animal Seeks Physical Contact

Physical contact is not necessarily required when it comes to Reiki Treatment. However, the same is important if the animal goes out of its way to seek the same. In case you notice that your animal is coming close to you to initiate physical contact during the Reiki treatment process, then you must go ahead and provide such contact in order for the treatment to be effective.

Chapter 3: Benefits of Reiki

Reiki has many benefits, including healing the body, mind, and spirit but it also helps promote balance and harmony both within the body and our environment. Reiki is a non-invasive healing energy that helps enhance and promote the body's natural healing abilities while encouraging the flow of Ki which overall enhances the body's wellbeing. Reiki can restore balance on all levels within the body and it can directly heal the problem instead of just taking away the pain or relieving some symptoms.

In terms of balance, Reiki can create an emotional and mental balance between the good and the bad. When healing the body from its problem, you are putting less stress on the mind, which affects the mental and emotional state of the human brain. Balance comes from when a person is able to live free from any worries about their own bodies. When there is no stress, there is no anger meaning many negative feelings simply fade away, leaving the body with a balanced and harmonized mindset. Reiki has also the power to heal depression, anxiety, negative emotions, and many other mental illnesses.

Reiki can also relieve any tension within the body and stress itself. When the treatment is in process, Reiki doesn't just go through a particular part of the body that has a problem, it might start with that part, but it makes itself flow all throughout the body, relaxing it and releasing of any stress and tension. Many practitioners reported feeling relaxed, clear-minded, lighter, and peaceful after performing Reiki on themselves or after Reiki has been done on them. This is because the energy flows everywhere, releasing tension that has been put on any parts within your body.

Many of today's known diseases are linked to a stress factor such as work stress, environmental stress, or even emotional stress. This leads to irregular heart rhythms that can cause a stroke, angina, gastrointestinal problems, eating disorders, mood disorders, sexual problems, and many psychological problems. Reiki can help you regulate this stress to avoid any problems within the mind and body.

You are able to achieve natural balance with the body, mind, and spirit due to Reiki dissolving any chakra or energy blocks. These energy blocks can also affect the body physically or mentally. When Reiki is done regularly, it can bring a more peaceful and calmer state to the body and person who is dealing with stress in their everyday lives. The mental balance can also enhance mental clarity, memory, and learning, as well as heal emotional or mental wounds, frustrations, anger, mood swings, fear, and even personal relationships. In general, Reiki enhances your ability to give love and receive love, making you more open to any people and relationships around you.

Reiki is able to give one space where they are able to become more aware of what is happening within their bodies, causing them to make decisions that change the way they live their lives in terms of diet, habits, etc. Many practitioners even report changing their habits or abandoning them. When you become more present of what is happening within your body, you start to access inner wisdom or knowledge. It changes your point of view on certain things in your environment or life.

We are so easily affected by the stress we experience every day in our lives that sometimes it even becomes our 'normal,' and our bodies completely forget what it's like to be in balance once again. Many practitioners can tell you that Reiki is a wonderful and gentle healing practice that makes their body and mind feel amazing, that is the body's true, normal, and balanced nature. It can be rather difficult to maintain this balance but that is why Reiki can be practiced regularly to ensure the body is able to return to its balanced state. Reiki is able to remind our body how to shift into its own self-healing mode even when Reiki is not being practiced. This parasympathetic nervous system state allows you to digest and sleep better, which is very important when it comes to the body's health and vitality. The more often you are able to achieve this state, the more you can become productive and active without the feelings of exhaustion, stress, or burnout floating inside you.

Reiki improves your connection to the Universe and nature. It also has the power to ground and center you by improving focus within the mind. With the help of this energy and your mind, you will be able to stay centered in this present moment instead of living in the past and always being stopped by guilt and regrets from moving on and living your best life. Reiki can help strengthen the ability that revolves around accepting yourself and any events that happen around you, even if they are not aligned with your desires or goals. Instead of acting out of habit, you are able to be more supportive of yourself and others around you; Reiki can help you look at the brighter things when life throws you challenges.

As mentioned above, Reiki can promote better relaxation, which aids in better sleep. With sleep and relaxed bodies, the healing process can go by more smoothly and at a faster rate. You are also able to think more clearly, become focused, and move forward on your spiritual path. This deep relaxation releases many tensions within the body, making it finally function smoothly which is different from your old toxic and tense body. Many practitioners who practice Reiki on themselves or during their attunement, report falling into a deep sleep due to the deep relaxation they experience.

After Reiki has been performed, your body goes to your natural state, accelerating the self-healing ability drastically. During this period, your heart rate, blood pressure, and breathing improve. You will be able to inhale and exhale more deeply and easier than before, this is usually one of the first things that show improvement after performing Reiki on yourself or when someone does Reiki on you. Deep breathing naturally settles our minds, and oxygen also helps fight cancer!

A Reiki treatment is able to restore balance on a very deep level, encouraging the system to improve the body's vital functions such as sleeping, breathing, and digesting. On a more physical level, Reiki is able to relieve the pain and symptoms of sciatica, migraines, arthritis, asthma, menopausal symptoms, chronic fatigue, insomnia, and many other illnesses. Reiki can also help stimulate and increase mobility in many cases of lower back pain, wrist pain, and shoulder pain. It also has the power to heal inflammations and infections within the body. Reiki, done on yourself or sent to someone over distance healing, has proven to work efficiently as told by many of those who received Reiki and perform Reiki on others. It can also improve indices of the metabolic syndrome which is associated with a risk of type two diabetes, many chronic conditions, and even heart disease.

Not only does Reiki cleanse the body physically, but spiritually too. Cleansing both the mind and body helps promote spiritual growth and personal development. Although you do not need to be spiritual to receive Reiki, it does help in your spiritual path. Instead of targeting individual symptoms, Reiki goes through the entire body. Often a practitioner receives messages, change of attitude, visions, or see things from a different point of view. It makes you see your condition in a new light and makes you deal with it in another and more positive way.

When one is relaxed, the healing process is accelerated. Reiki is a very gentle treatment that can be used on medical conditions such as diabetes, heart conditions, epilepsy, and many others. Reiki also supports chemotherapy. Reiki can also support women on any stage during their pregnancy and gives them the energy to carry on their day-to-day activities.

Many people often replace therapy with a Reiki practice, which is able to give you more self-love, enable you to connect with people on a more emotional level, strengthen your relationships, and solve problems that occur outside of your body. The way we think and what intentions we set for ourselves affect the environment around us; for example, when someone is always angry, their environment will be full of negative energy which can attract many problems and disappointment instead of desires and goals. Having clean thoughts and mindset can help you achieve your goals, Reiki can do that and so much more!

We've discussed the many benefits of this pure Universal healing energy, but there are also some negative effects that you should be aware of.

Reiki heals very fast, sometimes even way too quickly. Especially when it comes to healing emotional traumas or mental disorders, there are always negative feelings that occupy our thoughts. Many people go through something called the 'healing crisis,' which is a phase of the body in which the self-healing process started to work by vanishing any negativity and stress out of the system. In order for anyone to move on from something that is bothering them, either mentally or physically, one must first accept and acknowledge the situation. This is what happens in the 'healing crisis,' the energy acknowledges what the issue is and started to remove it from your system. Sometimes this healing process works way too fast, releasing emotions that you've been holding on for quite some time in order to heal yourself on a deeper level.

It's the same concept as fevers. When the body senses a virus from the outside of the body, it raises the temperature drastically, giving one fever and killing that virus in the process. The body just releases all that energy and emotions all at once, and for those who suffered very painful past traumas, it can be a very poor experience having all those emotions back up and running through your head. Many practitioners or clients report crying or yelling a lot during this time, but one shouldn't let these emotions get the better of them. It's simply the final step to releasing the negativity and moving on. Don't get too attached to that moment in your past but think of it as a challenge in life that you have overcome.

It is also not recommended to use Reiki for healing broken bones. Since Reiki is fast healing energy, broken bones might heal the wrong way and will require breaking them again for them to heal in the right direction. Reiki is a pure form of healing energy unless the practitioner or Reiki master uses the energy in the wrong way; there are no serious side effects.

On a more mental level, Reiki can help reduce anxiety and depression by changing your mood. When you feel more relaxed and less stressed, you feel more calm and happy about yourself and your environment, but when you are angry, you often take this feeling out on yourself and others around you. Changes in mood are associated with depression and anxiety. Many studies have proven that there is an overall improvement to one's mood after Reiki, these improvements lead to a reduction of confusion, fear, doubt, depression, anger, and anxiety in many practitioners. Loss of vigor, which is one of the symptoms of depression, returns to its original state once depression dissolves, which then improves the body's mental state.

Overcoming anxiety and reducing negative thoughts is the goal of a healthy body. A research study published in 2006 had a goal determining if Reiki can actually reduce anxiety in women who were experiencing hysterectomies. Those who received the Reiki treatments experienced having a drastic reduction in anxiety than those who were in the control groups. This study, however, only applied to women who were undergoing surgery. Another research carried in Turkey wanted to determine whether Reiki treatment can reduce pain, fatigue, and anxiety among cancer patients. The study found that those who had a Reiki treatment done on them had experienced a reduction and improvement in all these variables. Another different study aimed to discover where treating older adults would improve their anxiety, depression, and some other issues. Yet again, the results didn't disappoint. Many participants of that study reported that not only did their symptoms fade away, but they experienced complete relaxation during a Reiki treatment.

It is safe to say that you, too, can heal your anxiety and many other issues with the help of Universal life energy. But first things first, you must learn a bit more about this amazing and pure energy before jumping into the healing process. Reiki isn't just done on oneself but it can be performed on others too, such as people, animals, events, and plants.

Self-healing is the most popular practice. There are many different ways and techniques of one performing Reiki on themselves. This works by using your hands and placing them in a certain position above countless parts of your body, from top to bottom to ensure that the energy travels everywhere.

Hands-on-healing is the most basic form of healing that revolves around giving the healing energy to someone who is physically present with you. You ask the person to lie down in order for them to relax completely, with their eyes closed and in a comfortable position. The healing begins with the practitioner's hands hovering above the crown chakra and making their way throughout the other chakras in the patient's body.

Distant healing involves a practitioner performing Reiki on another that is not physically present in the moment. When performing distant healing, you must ask the person to have some time to themselves to relax, sit down with their eyes closed and legs crossed for a couple of minutes while you perform the Reiki healing. Reiki can also be done on those who don't believe in the process or those who never had Reiki done on them before. Reiki can also be done to those who are unaware that this process is happening to them. Distant healing energy can also be sent using object forms, such as a photograph or an image of them, an intention slip, or an object that belongs to them.

Distant healing can also be used for occasions or events such as healing broken relationships or sending love and healing to families who are going through tough times. Reiki can be used on past events such as heartbreak or childhood traumas. Reiki doesn't have the power to change the past, but it can help you move on and change the way you feel about that event. Such as changing fear into strength.

Reiki can also be used on other living things such as plants and animals. Applying the same hands-on-healing but slightly changing your intentions can help. For an animal or pet that requires healing, simply focus and hover your hands around the animal. It can be difficult for them to stay still, which is why it is best given when the animal is asleep. For plants, sending Reiki through roots to promote faster and stronger growth, it can also be used on soil, water, seeds.

Reiki helps the body in self-purification, thus promoting immunity. There are much energy and time needed to fight stress and its causes that dictate the nature of lives. At long last, we forget to balance our lives. Our bodies are tuned to the game of stress management naturally until there is no room for relaxation. When Reiki comes in, it acts as a sympathizer that brings us to rest so that we can experience a moment of healing. At this stage, you will still remain active as usual and much productive. The difference will be that your body will be given more room to rest and meditate which is essential for body health and strength. When you allow Reiki in your life, it makes life more productive and active, free from stress and exhaustion or depletion.

Frees Up the Mindset, Makes You More Focused, Rooted, and Stable. You will remain composed and in a steadier condition as opposed to, overthinking over the past events, or even worrying for the future unknowns. Reiki lets you live today as a day and not live in the past or the future. At the end of the day, you will feel sober even when the conditions are not favorable to you, especially in your work environment. Instead of allowing the situations to control you, you will be in a position to challenge them and stand out as strong as if there was no challenge at all. You will end up being of great help to others who feel low or weak as a result of stress or de-motivation.

Chapter 4: The Reiki Symbols

Usui Reiki symbols are very sacred and are usually only used by those who have been attuned to the Reiki Second or Third degree. They are also to be kept confidential. These symbols are known to be very powerful which makes them important and a huge part of a Reiki practice. They focus the energy of Reiki on a specific point, for example, if sending healing through a distance, the Distance Symbol is used to enhance the focus and power for it to be more efficient. In the Usui Reiki system, there are a total of four main symbols in which three are given during Reiki II and one is given in Reiki III. There are also other symbols than many practitioners and Master's use but they are not part of the Usui system but will still be discussed below.

These symbols have emerged from a Japanese kanji, which is actually just words from the Japanese language. Although the symbol names can be translated from Japanese to English dictionary, the symbols themselves are a mix of Japanese and Sanskrit kanji. This practice originated from Japanese Buddhists' who, many times, combined the Japanese kanji with the ancient Sanskrit within their sacred symbols and writings. The symbols in the Usui system and those symbols that are outside of the system may have been influenced by this ancient practice. Only the Power and the Mental/Emotional symbols are a mix of Sanskrit and Japanese kanji while the Master and Distance symbols are fully Japanese kanji. Both their characters and their names can be found within an English/Japanese dictionary.

In the past, the Reiki symbols have been kept a secret in order to honor their sacredness. But there is a reason behind that when keeping the power of the Reiki symbols a secret; one is maintaining its sacred connection. Many teachers and Masters of Reiki reveal the symbols only after the attunement process and after teaching them about the new degree of Reiki in order for them to not feel misguided and give them the correct knowledge of Reiki.

Most of the Reiki symbols have some effect on the practitioner's subconscious mind, creating a somewhat of a change inside the practitioner's internal state, however because of this, the Reiki symbols can access the source from where Reiki is located within the practitioner's body and signal that change in terms of how the Reiki energy works free from the practitioner's internal state. These symbols can be activated in many ways, such as by calling out their names, visualizing them, or drawing them with your hand either in the air, on your palm, or on a piece of paper. Many practitioners like to combine all of the above by drawing the symbol, visualizing it, and saying its name three times in order to activate it. Just thinking of the symbol during the Reiki process can activate it. The link of the symbols comes from the attunement process; you will not be able to use the Reiki symbols without it.

There are many other symbols that are used by different practitioners in different treatments, but these are the most common and ancient ones that have been passed down generations.

The Power symbol

The first Reiki symbol is the Power symbol, which is only available after the completion of Reiki II attunement. This symbol, known as Choku Rei (Cho-Koo-Ray), translates to 'Place the power of the universe here.' Just like it's general meaning, this symbol can be used to increase the energy and power of Reiki during a healing practice. It works like a light switch, turn it on and your ability and power of channeling Reiki energy immediately boosts. Additionally, it can be used to protect oneself.

Many practitioners also believe that one has already received the power symbol during the Reiki I attunement, and there are some practitioners who can use the Power symbol during their first degree in Reiki. If you do decide to use the Choku Rei symbol, first make sure that you have practiced the Reiki treatment on yourself a couple of times in order to not be overwhelmed by the energy that the Power symbol gives.

This Reiki symbol works as an enhancement of the power and ability of the Reiki healing energy; you can use this to your advantage. If you have something specific that you want the Reiki energy to do, you can use the Power symbol and combine it with your intention or a clear declaration of what you want the symbol to do, and it will do it. Some practitioners used the power symbol to increase the energy of the following:

- Healing power abilities by visualizing or drawing the Power symbol on the hands.
- Spiritual cleansing from any negative energy or turn it into a sacred space by visualizing or drawing the symbol on all of the walls, the floor, and the ceiling, it can also be used to energize the room before a Reiki session.
- Cleansing crystals from negative energies by drawing the power symbol in the air above the crystal to cleanse it, then hold it with both of your hands and give some Reiki healing to the crystal, it can also be done on different objects.
- Healing injuries, pains, or aches by drawing the symbol above the area.
- Increasing the power of other symbols by drawing the Power symbol before other symbols.

- Heal a specific point of the body, focusing that energy at that point by drawing the symbol above that part of your body.
- Sealing the healing session in order to stop the energies from disappearing from one's body by drawing the symbol above the body in the air with the correct intention.
- Protection from negative energies such as people or entities, simply draw the symbol in the air in front of you with the intention of protection from negativity, it can also be drawn on other people, houses, animals, and children in order to protect them.
- Healing relationships, direct the Power symbol on the person who you wish to heal the relationship with, they don't have to be physically present with you.
- There are many other uses in which the Power symbol holds; you can also use your own imagination and intuition to use the Power symbol for other things.

How to use Choku Rei

When using this symbol, your visualization and intention skills are important. Many practitioners use this symbol at the beginning of a Reiki session; it is important you are able to focus and put your intention through it.

Simply by calling out the symbols name, visualizing it or drawing it in front of you is all it takes to activate the Power symbol. Although the symbol can be used any time during the practice, activating it before you begin the Reiki treatment is more beneficial to empower the Reiki energy throughout the session. It can also be used at the end of the treatment, in order to seal away the Reiki energies and close off the session. Sometimes one would need to draw the symbol directly over the area in the body in which will require healing instead of saying it out loud to enhance the power of Reiki.

The horizontal line is associated with the Reiki source within your body while the vertical line represents the energy flow. The spiral symbolizes the seven chakras as it touches the middle line seven times. To draw it, first, draw the horizontal line, then the vertical line, and then the spirals. The Choku Rei spiral is supposed to be drawn from left to right, anticlockwise but many people prefer drawing it clockwise. Follow your intuition and figure out which works better for you.

The Mental/Emotional symbol

The Mental/Emotional symbol is the second symbol, which is mainly used in Reiki II and Reiki III. This symbol is called Sei He Ki (Say-Hay-Key) and it means 'God and Man become one.' Just like its general meaning, this symbol brings together the body and the mind, uniting them and making them one. Since the mind is such a powerful being itself and can even control the body in a good and bad way, it is often associated with the Higher Self, or also known as God. The body represents the Man and together, they unite and become one. This symbol helps to bring those two together as well as releasing any emotional or mental causes of the practitioner's problems.

As known by many people, doctors, and science itself, the mental state of one person causes problems from within the body. The imbalance found within the emotional and mental state can cause harm to the human body since the mind controls it. If the mind is polluted, then the body will not function properly. This symbol can help harmonize and focus the subconscious mind with the physical part of oneself.

This symbol is used to help with mental and emotional healing, illnesses within the mind, such as depression, anxiety, stress, and many others. It helps the mind by balancing the right and the left side of the brain in order to bring harmony and peace to the body. Many times this symbol has been used to cure relationship problems and on diverse problems such as nervousness, anger, and fear. Some practitioners used the mental/emotional symbol to increase the energy of the following:

- It can also be used to lose weight, simply by drawing the symbol in front of one's body or saying them out loud with the correct intentions in mind.
- When studying, use Sei He Ki to improve your memory by drawing the symbol on the page that you are trying to memorize or learn for a test. It will help you remember the important parts.
- Healing addiction has to do with alcohol, drugs, or smoking by setting an intention and drawing the symbol in front of one's head, where the mind is.
- This symbol can aid in finding misplaced things by drawing it in front of you and asking for help to find whatever you are missing, let go of looking for the object, and trying to find it. It will turn up when you least expect it.

- When performing a healing treatment, this symbol can help improve the rate of the healing process since many physical problems come from the mind.

How to use Sei He Ki

Simply activating it before a session is how you improve the healing treatment, especially when it's distance related. The intention is also quite important to this symbol since it relates to the balance of the mind, just like the Yin and Yang.

Sei-He-Kei

The left part of the symbol is associated with the left side of our brain, the Yang, which represents the structure, clear thinking, and logic. The right side of the symbol is associated with the right side of the brain, the Yin, which represents intuition, feelings, and fantasy. When drawing this symbol on yourself, simply begin with the left side, making your way down and then proceed to the line on the right, and finishing with the two semicircles. When drawing this symbol on another person and you are facing them face-to-face, the left side symbol ends up on the receiver's right side while the right side ends up on the left.

The Distance Symbol

The third symbol is the Distance healing symbol, which is only used by practitioners on Reiki II and Reiki III. This symbol is called Hon Sha Ze ShoNen (Hon-Sha-Zee-Show-Nen) and it means 'No past, no present, no future,' and it also has the meaning of 'The Buddha in me contacts the Buddha in you.' The Distance symbol is mainly used to help sent healing and energy over a distance to someone who is not physically present with you. Distance and time is not a problem for the Universe, especially when it comes to using this Reiki symbol.

The Hon Sha Ze ShoNen is known to be a very powerful and useful symbol out of all for its ability to even access the 'Akashic Records,' which are the life records of each soul. This can be used to one's advantage when it comes to karmic healing. Experiences or traumas from either this life, past life, or a parallel life are what affects peoples' behaviors in this current moment. The Hon Sha Ze ShoNen symbol can help heal that and so many more things. There is always a root experience to anxiety which has occurred in the past, sending Reiki to that event can help you move on and heal from anxiety.

When doing distance healing, don't focus on a specific problem of that person but instead send the Reiki energy to heal anything and everything, let the Universe guide the energy where its best needed. This symbol can be used on those who do not know that Reiki healing is being sent to them; this is useful for those who are in critical conditions or in hospitals. If the person is well and either aware or not that Reiki healing is being sent to them, then it is most likely that the person will be able to feel its energy when it is happening. If that person has an open mind, they will be able to tell exactly when and what you have done.

The distance symbol sends the energy to the receiver's body and works with the aura and the chakras, but not that much when it comes to the physical level. This also means that it will take some time for the receiver to feel an ease with the pain or for the healing to 'kick in.' Distance healing requires a few minutes to successfully send it but it doesn't take as long as a common hands-on treatment. It is even possible to set Reiki distance healing to automatic repeat, meaning it will send the Reiki healing energy every day but it is important to set a preferred time limit and renew and empower the healing energy every other day in order for it to be efficient. Follow your intuition and let it guide you. Some practitioners used the distance symbol to help with the following:

- Sending Reiki healing energy to the future in order to help with a specific event or task or provide comfort and support by drawing the symbol in the air or on a specific object that will relate to the future.
- Sending Reiki healing energy to people in different places all around the world by drawing a symbol in front of their picture.
- Sending Reiki healing energy to the past in order to be free from traumas and move on by drawing or calling out the symbol's name.

How to use Hon Sha Ze ShoNen

Every time the Distance symbol is used, it is important for you to give clear intentions and direct the Reiki to a specific receiving source, either a physical person or event. Visualization also plays an important role in this symbol, instead of using a picture of the one you want to heal, you can simply visualize the person in your head. Imagine the person you want to heal and then proceed by sending the energy to them. Using a picture can help you focus more and its best for those who do not have great visualization skills.

Many times Masters send Reiki through the Distance symbol to a person that only provided their name and the city in which they reside, it is not the information that matters but the intention of sending the healing energy to this unknown person. This is the most complex Reiki symbol but it is easy to use once one has understood how. The power of intention is important in all symbols, but this one holds more importance. Intentions are like directions sent for the Reiki energy to follow; without it, the Reiki energy will not know where to go.

This is a powerful symbol and has to be used correctly in order for it to work. It is recommended that one practices how to draw the symbol properly before jumping into performing any treatments. The symbol symbolizes the human body combining the five elements and the chakras together. In order for this symbol to provide efficient energy, one must call it on a day-to-day basis in order to encourage the future and past healing within the body.

The Master Symbol

The fourth and the last main Reiki symbol is the Master symbol, which can only be used by practitioners who have been attuned to the Reiki III degree. This symbol is called Dai Ko Myo (Dye-Ko-My-O) and it means 'bright shining light' and 'great enlightenment.' This symbol has the highest vibrations which is why it is used at the highest Reiki level to ensure that those who call on the symbol will be able to handle its overwhelming energy and power because the energy is sent to the upper chakras and the subtle layer of one's aura. This symbol can help enhance the healing within one's soul on a very high spiritual level; once the soul is healed, both the physical and the mental states get healed immediately.

The Master symbol can also help heal karma; it is known for its 'all-purpose healing' and represents all Reiki, love, and empowerment. Although practitioners at all degrees have already received the master symbol, it is suggested for it to only be used once one reaches the Reiki III. The Dai Ko Myo is the most sacred symbol out of all; it is enlightening and nourishing and many of those who received a treatment involving the Master symbol report feeling as if one just met their Higher Self or God after the treatment has been performed. This symbol brings the practitioners closer to God and faith.

The Master symbol encourages self-purification and self-cleansing at a spiritual level; it can also create a balance and harmony within one's life. This symbol is responsible for making you see the brighter things in life as if bringing 'light' into your life. The Dai Ko Myo symbol can help eliminate blockages within the emotional, physical, mental, or spiritual level in your past, present, or future. This symbol can be used for the following:

- Healing the seven chakras, any diseases within the mind, the aura, and many others that are associated with the subconscious mind.
- Increase in psychic abilities and intuition by drawing the symbol in front of the practitioner or receiver with the correct intention.
- Increase in the strength within one's spiritual development, personal growth, intuition, and self-awareness.
- Healing or eliminating past traumas.

- Strengthening your relationship with yourself, such as self-love or self-respect.
- Strengthening, clearing blockages, and improving the immune system by activating this symbol's energy to flow through the entire body.
- Enhancing the healing properties found within homeopathic remedies such as essential oils or homemade ointments.
- Helping Reiki Masters by opening the channels in the receiver during a Reiki attunement.
- Cleansing or charging crystals by simply drawing the symbol above the crystal and meditating with it in both your hands.

How to use Dai Ko Myo

In order to call on this powerful and sacred symbol, one must draw the symbol and visualize it or draw it using your third eye. Mediations with this symbol can also help receive its power and will help you access it more efficiently in the future.

The 'Dai' means big or great, like the energy received while 'Ko' means glossy or smooth. The word 'Myo' means bright light which signifies the light coming into one's life. This symbol is also an 'empowerment' symbol. It also represents enlightenment, truth, and inner knowledge.

The Completion Symbol

The completion symbol is not part of the Usui Reiki system, but it is used by many practitioners to this day. The Japanese name for the completion symbol is Raku (Ra-Koo) which means 'fire serpent.' It is used for grounding after a Reiki treatment has been performed. This symbol allows the practitioner to receive all the benefits of Reiki once it is drawn from the head and to the ground. This symbol is also used to clear any negative energy from the person that the practitioner was performing Reiki on.

Mainly used at the end of a Reiki practice, this symbol can be used on the practitioner as a protection from negative energy and on the receiver to ensure all the healing energy has been transferred and stored within the receiver's body. This symbol is drawn like a lightning bolt, starting from the top and making the way to the bottom.

Many of the Reiki symbols have very strong properties, which can help enhance the power of a Reiki healing treatment, but many of those symbols can also be used multiple times throughout the session. These Reiki symbols do not have to be used alone; in fact, they should be accompanied by other symbols to ensure absolute success. Many times, practitioners use multiple symbols to help treat and heal a sick child using Reiki. For example, visualizing the Power symbol, the Mental/Emotional symbol, the Distance symbol, and the Power symbol one by one, three times each. Hold the picture of the sick child with repeating their name three times to help you focus, is also used to center the energy and concentration through the session.

That is just one example out of many when more than one symbol can be used. Like mentioned earlier, there is no time plane when it comes to Reiki. For example, if you are worried and nervous about an event and you believe that it may bring bad news or disappointment in the future, simply use Reiki to help you seek a positive outcome out of what is about to happen. Saying the following names Cho Ku Rei, Sei He Ki, Hon Sha Ze ShoNen, and Cho Ku Rei about three times each, or visualizing their corresponding symbols while setting an intention to bring a calming and peaceful outcome for that day. This will surely bring you positive and peaceful vibrations when the event comes. You will feel more relaxed and mentally stable which are the requirements for dealing with a situation in a positive manner.

Don't be afraid to experiment with different symbol combinations and follow your intuition. Everyone is different and holds a different Reiki energy capacity which all depends on one's vibrational state. Follow your intuition and remember that the more you practice Reiki, the easier and more efficiently you will be able to channel the energy.

Chapter 5: Reiki and Body Energy

Everything is about energy, which means that healing also ultimately involves energy. In Reiki, energy helps promote healing through enhancing the flow of energy and correcting any disturbances that occur in the "human energy field," also called the aura. This aura permeates the body and surrounds it. When the body experiences the flow of energy, the body will have the capacity to heal by itself.

Energy healing works on the basis that your body is made up of various patterns of energy. When you work directly with body energy, you will influence the mental, physical, and emotional level. Using energy healing in Reiki is seen to be holistic in nature.

This is why it is vital that when your body or mind experiences disturbances, everyone wants to address these levels. However, energy healing doesn't work on its own; rather, it supports other healing methods that we use in daily life. Reiki healing focuses on the energy of which your body, mind, and emotions are made up of.

At the center of the human field are seven primary chakras that are supported by thousands of other smaller meridians and chakras. The seven chakras are placed in a vertical manner along your spinal column, and it begins on the pelvic floor. The first one is the Root chakra that is at the level of the pelvic bone, and the one at the top is the Crown chakra. Each of the chakras works as its own transmitter as well as the recipient of the energy. When the chakra receives the energy, it will direct it to corresponding organs as well as the endocrine system within the body.

The Energetic Bodies

In addition to the chakra, the human body uses the human energy field to make it work perfectly. The energy field is made up of smaller energetic bodies, which include the mental, spiritual, etheric, emotional, and physical bodies. All these allow you to relate with and experience the environment in different aspects.

When all the chakras and energy bodies are in harmony and are working well together, you will be full of vitality and have a sense of wellness. On the other hand, when the energy centers are not balanced, you will become sluggish, and you will experience confusion, fatigue, and illness at all times. You need to work with a healing practice that can identify the problem areas. He will do so with the aim of releasing the blockages then create a positive flow of energy in the body so that he can make you heal. Healing can happen immediately, or it can take time.

The 5 Layers of the Human Energy Field

As described earlier, the human energy field is composed of 5 layers that we explore below:

Physical Energy

This is the layer that we look at to be the physical part of ourselves. Although we look at the body as a package that consists of the skin, flesh, bones, and organs, they also have energy, similar to the other layers of the body that you can't see, or you cannot sense such as the mind.

Etheric

This word is derived from the word "ether," – which is a layer that sits from one quarter to one half of an inch, but not any more than an inch, from the location of the physical body. The practitioners that have sensed this body describe it as a feeling that is gray in color. It is like a spider web, and it can stretch, and it is usually seen as the blueprint of the physical layer.

Emotional Energy

This is the third layer from the outside. It is at the center of all the five layers that we have looked at. The emotional layer is the layer where fears and feelings reside. It can be very volatile when we have emotions. It comes into play whether you are experiencing both low and high emotions.

Mental Energy

This is the layer where our ideas and other emotions spring from. It also forms the store from which the belief system gets stored. This is the space where our thoughts are stored then sorted out, and it is where people store their personal truths or any perceptions that are based on experiences.

Spiritual Energy

This is the final layer, where higher awareness and consciousness is stored. It is the layer where our past lives are tied as well as the universal consciousness that is common to all people.

Why Should You Be Concerned About Energy Field?

Studies show that the main factor that will limit you is the low-frequency energies that you have stored within your body. You need to be aware that the personal energy field has a huge impact on the general sense of well-being. People are usually aware of how important personal hygiene is. You need to know that the physical body gets dirty when you use it, and it can pick up viruses and bacteria that can lead to disease. So, if you stop looking after your body, your physical health, as well as a sense of well-being, will also suffer.

Have you ever felt that your state of mind feels "dirty" when your body is dirty as well? This is because everything that you do is connected to the energy, which also means that every part of your life comes with an energy component. Visible dirt is just a part of the bigger problem. Any part of your body is made up of many energy frequencies, most that cannot be seen with the naked eye. However, you need to know that the unseen energy frequencies will affect the energy field as well.

The major problem that we face is that we have grown up in a society that doesn't acknowledge the unseen energies and how they are important to our lives. In school, we are only taught about the energies that we can see, and how they affect our lives, we aren't taught about what we cannot see.

For you to understand how it all works, you need to look at all the five layers of the human energy fields. It is a fact that for you to have total body hygiene, you ought to keep all the five layers of body energy clean. When you have knowledge about the different fields, you will be able to know that the conditions in your body that you think is caused by physical causes might be due to energy imbalance. You don't need to limit yourself at a single part of the body; rather, you need to look at the different layers before you make any conclusion. So, if you wish to handle the proper healing of the body, you need to do so by working at all the layers of the body.

Energy Healing: What You Need to Know

When you go through the paces of energy healing, you need to make sure that you understand what has been done before and what else needs to be done. Here are the top things that you need to understand about energy healing:

1. It has Been Studied for Many Years

Reiki has been used in traditional Japanese medicine for many years. Additionally, Chakras have been described in ancient

Hindu scripts. Acupuncture uses the meridians to find healing power. We can see that ancient cultures used these different modalities to stimulate your body's natural ability to heal and be better. They identified internal energy as the best way to heal the whole body.

2. It Is Based on Science

In physics class in high school, we learned that matter is composed of molecules that are in constant motion. Even something that is as solid as a rock is also vibrating continuously. People that have a fulfilling life vibrate at a higher frequency compared to people with low frequency. Places also have vibration frequencies as well. When the place has a vibe, it will either give you a positive or a negative vibe as well. Places that have a negative vibe will make it impossible for you to be in the space for long. For instance, air at the beach is at a higher frequency, which makes it easy for you to sit and relax.

3. Energy Healing Is for Everyone

You don't need to grasp the concept of energy healing in order for you to enjoy the benefits. When you decide to try it out, make sure you go with an open mind so that you enjoy all the benefits. You can visit an energy healer any time you like. If you are anxious or stressed, a session with an energy healer is ideal for you. The session will help you feel more balanced and relax, as well. If you are already feeling so good, you will get to feel better when you use the method of energy healing. However, we need to stress that energy healing is an alternative form of healing. You need to combine it with other conventional medical procedures to achieve total healing.

4. It Is Accessible

You can work with Reiki healers the world over. Many people think that Reiki healers are just confined to a certain part of the world, but this is a wrong notion. The truth is that you can get a healer right to your doorstep; all you need to do is to find a way to link up with them. Do you know that you can make use of Reiki healing even without meeting the healer face to face? Yes, it is true. All you need to know is that the power of Reiki can make the energy to flow to where it is required. For the most part, you need to get referrals from people that have used the practice before for it to be successful. Ask a friend who is into energy healing or ask your yoga master at the studio for referrals.

5. You Can Connect with Your Inner Self at Home

Just the way you wake up each morning and brush your teeth, you can also make healing your daily habit so that you enjoy the various benefits. Once you have a session with the energy healer, you can keep the energy flowing by using homemade energy healing remedies such as taking a bath with Epsom salts each day. All you need to experience the healing powers of your energy is to be willing to learn and to start on the journey to wellness.

Chapter 6: Beginner Reiki Meditation

How to Create the Best Self-Reiki Practice

Now that you have learned the various levels of Reiki healing, it is time to get into the swing of things. You will find it easier to run the life the way it needs to be run, and you will be able to enjoy your tasks each day. However, you need to come up with the right schedule so that you can incorporate Reiki into your daily routine. The good thing is that all you need to enjoy Reiki self-healing is yourself – nothing else. Here are a few tips to get you running:

Start Small

For you to enjoy the benefits of Reiki, it is advisable that you start off small. You might choose to do 30 minutes a day after the first meeting with the practitioner, but you will definitely find this to be hard. Our busy lives don't allow us to do this. Make sure you set a time duration that you can stick to. If you choose to do 10 minutes a day, then be it. If you feel you can only handle 5 minutes, then go for it. Just make sure you start small then build upon what you have started. Gradually build up the time, and soon, you will be able to do more.

Make it a Daily Routine

The more consistent you are to self-healing practices, the easier it will be for you. Make sure you are consistent in all you do and believe in what you are doing to make sure you achieve your goals. Consistent daily sessions will give you a better result than long term sporadic sessions. Just the way you set a routine for going to the gym, you will find that setting a specific time of day for you to perform the self-practice will work better than if you decide to do things anytime you feel like. You will also find that getting a particular spot in the house of the task will make it ideal for you. Set up the spot in the same space each day so that you remember that you have a task to do. Early in the morning or late in the evening after work are the best times to handle the Reiki.

Know Why you are Into Reiki

You need to understand why you took up Reiki in the first place. Was it for relaxation, was it for healing? Was it to recover? Well, all in all, you need to understand the benefits that you stand to gain before you a start doing Reiki. Remember what you felt in the first session before you get into it. Mae sure you relate to the past successes so that you can use them for the present motivations. Imagine what you wish to achieve, then see what Reiki has done for you so far, then use this motivation to see how you will feel later on if you do the same routine. Make sure you connect to your benefits at all times so that you have a goal in mind at all times.

Understand the Limitations

When you try to create the perfect self-practice, you might have to remind yourself why you decided to go for Reiki in the first instance. Remind yourself of the various consequences that might happen when you fail to do Reiki. For instance, your worry might grow. Try to know the reasons why you took up Reiki in the first place and what you will lose if you give it up.

Use a Guide

You need to have a guided meditation so that you don't get distracted at all. Many times our minds are too busy to focus on the meditation practice, but with guided meditation, you will be able to keep your mind on many things. You can also set a timer so that it goes off in a few minutes so that you can move to the next position. You can also use mantras so that you can focus your mind on a single object.

Lower Expectations

What are your expectations when you get into a session? Are you out to improve the existing session or you just want to get something out of it? Either way, you need to come up with goals and make sure you follow them to the latter. Many people think that they have their goals well set out only to discover later that they don't have anything.

Reiki on the Go

You don't have to be in a single position to enjoy Reiki. What you need to know is that you can perform Reiki whenever and wherever you can. People have gone to the extent of performing healing sessions on a plane, or deep in the mountains. Either way, they get the same feeling that they get when they are in a setup position. The aim of self-healing is not to show anything rather be at peace with ourselves.

Believe You Can

Anyone can learn the basics of Reiki and use them to make their life easier. Regardless of age, personality, and history, you can still make sense of Reiki. However, many people think that they can't do it, and this is why they never even try to.

Repeat Until You Achieve Your Goals

People will fall off the wagon time and again. If you have ever done self Reiki, then you know that you will stop every time and then start again. If you stop and instead of picking yourself up, you end up stopping forever, then you will fail. Stopping is normal, and when you do, the way you regain your speed is what matters a lot.

When first starting off Reiki healing practice for the first time, it is important that you get used to the energy that you are harnessing before jumping into healing yourself. Reiki has very powerful energy; if one is not used to this energy, then one can experience negative side effects.

Begin by getting comfortable, preferably in an environment that makes you feel safe and has a special place in your heart. Common places such as the bedroom or the living room inside one's house are very beneficial. Keep in mind that whichever place you keep will be filled with your energy. Thus you must constantly meditate in the same place. It is important that your body can find peace and relaxation within that area, and so does your mind.

Turn off your phone and lock your doors; this way, you will not be disturbed. If you are able to hear some outside noises, you may want to consider putting some light instrumental music that can also be used to relax the body further. Beforehand, make sure that you wear loose clothing that can benefit you in terms of comfort.

Lay down on the place of your choosing and consider placing an extra pillow underneath your head or taking away the one that you already have, it will make it much harder for you to fall asleep if your mind slips away. Remember not to push yourself if you do manage to fall asleep, with practice and consistency; you can overcome that.

Take a breath in deeply through your nose, hold it for three seconds before breathing out through your mouth. Repeat the deep breathing for a couple more times, until you begin to feel your eyes wanting to close. Allow for your eyes to shut. As you breathe in, take notice of the way your chest rises and falls as you inhale and exhale. Set an intention for your body to relax, you can even declare it in your head if it's easier for you.

As your body falls into a state of relaxation, continue to paying close attention to your body moving as you breathe. Imagine your lungs expanding as you breathe in through your nose and shrinking as you breathe out through your mouth.

Begin to breathe like you normally do, and move your attention to your thoughts and your mind. Take a moment to clear away any thoughts that you might have or worries that might be clouding your mind, draining the focus from the sacral practice. Focus on the present, what is happening right now at this very moment and how you are letting go of any negative emotions. Push them aside and forget about them, you can worry about them later. What matters right now is receiving the healing that your body needs.

If you mind your mind wandering away to other places the first couple of minutes, then know that it is perfectly normal, that is the true nature of the mind. You will find other thoughts pop out in your head, but you also have the power to keep them at bay. When you realize that your mind has wandered off, bring your attention back to your breathing. Focus on the movement of your chest or any sensations that you might be experiencing all throughout your body.

You will feel your body reach its relaxational state, and you will know when is the right time to proceed. Imagine the Power symbol, Choku Rei, in your mind. It works like a light switch to help you harness and encourage the flow of Reiki within your body more effectively and easier. Take some time to visualize the symbol; focus on one right in front of you. When you start to see it clearly, take the extra step to visualize it once again. As many symbols as you can within your vision. You can even consider visualizing yourself in a white room, with countless power symbols drawn on the walls around you rather than just hanging in the air. Allow yourself to feel the power vibrating through the symbols. Hold the final image in your head for a couple of more seconds before proceeding.

Set an intention to harness the Reiki energy. Know that the Reiki energy is always within you; it's the life force energy that has been within your body ever since you got it. Focus on your body as a whole and allow the energy to resurface and flow throughout your body. Stay focused and calm as you will feel tingling sensations in different parts of your body; it is simply your body reacting to the energy.

As you let the energy simply flow within your body, you will begin to feel light, as if you are floating right above the place you are lying at. You will feel in touch with the energy within your body as if you are one. Continue by bringing your attention to the bottom of your body, the toes, and the feet. Let the flow of Reiki travel there, hovering around the area, healing it and energizing it. Let the energy rest there for ten seconds, or however, you feel fit before allowing it to travel further up. You will feel tingling sensations or an itch forming there, simply ignore it and remind yourself to not move.

Allow the energy to travel upwards, through your legs, hovering over specific areas that you feel need more attention, then allow the energy to travel higher, passing through your reproductive system, your stomach, and making it's way past your chest, your heart, all the way until the top of your head. Allow for the energy to rest there for a while, connecting with your mind and the subconscious before sending it to travel down your body, towards the very bottom where your toes are.

This simple practice allows for your body to get used to the energy as well as loosening any tense areas. Continue to focus on that energy traveling to the toes until it reaches there. Let it rest for a couple more seconds before allowing it to go back up to the top of your head. Continue following and encouraging the flow of Reiki through your body at least three times. You will feel your breath slowing down, and your body reaching its maximum relaxation state. Set intentions for your body to get used to channel this energy by imagining the power symbol once again, this time just floating above you. It's energy intervening with the Reiki healing energy, strengthening it, and energizing it.

Allow for your body to cleanse from any negativity by setting this intention on the last time you allow the life force to travel up and down your body. This pure energy can extinguish any negativity within your mind or body, and any tensions that you might be suffering from. Visualize letting go of any negativity by imagining breathing in pure energy as you breathe in. Allow for it to travel through your body, collecting all the negative energy and exiting it once you breathe out.

Once you are done, allow for the Reiki force energy to equally distributed throughout your body, just the way it was before you let it travel through your body. Visualize that energy hovering over your body, taking the same shape as you before falling into your body and settling in. Your physical body might feel heavier than before, and you will feel as if you are being sucked into the place in which you are lying.

Take a couple of minutes to settle in and return yourself back into the present moment. Allow for your mind to acknowledge what is happening right here and now by bringing your awareness to your chest rising and falling as you breathe in and out. Then bring your attention to your body, take notice of any tingling sensations that you might feel before bringing your attention to the way your body feels as it lays against the place of your choosing.

Continue breathing for another minute before proceeding by visualizing the Completion symbol, Raku, simply hovering above you. It's the energy of grounding falling onto your body, finalizing the Reiki meditation by sealing in the pure energy within your body, and protecting you from any negativity that might interfere. After visualizing the Completion symbol, take some time to relax and rest for a minute before allowing for your eyes to simply open.

Don't get up yet. Take some time to reflect on the Reiki meditation that you have experienced, take notice of how your body felt before the meditation and how it feels now. Rest for a minute, allowing the energy to settle in further before getting up. You might either feel tired from using so much energy or energized as if that energy is embodied right into your bones. Make sure to drink a cup of water after your meditation, to encourage the flow of energy and bring the body and mind back into its present state.

Chapter 7: Advanced Reiki Meditation

Emotional Healing Reiki Healing Meditation

Find a comfortable and safe place in your home to perform the self-treatment. It can be your bedroom, or living room, wherever you seem comfortable. Whichever space you pick, you will have to use it continuously if possible. These treatments can be performed on a bed, the floor, and the sofa while lying down or sitting in a chair if you'd like. Lock your doors, turn your phone on silent, and ask to be not disturbed during this time. It is recommended that you are alone during these self-treatments unless someone that you require to have someone in the room in order to make you feel safe and secure then you are welcome to bring them along. Just ask them to not speak or disturb you in any way.

When making your environment quiet and comforting, you can choose to play some music, not the kind that has lyrics; otherwise, you will find yourself singing along and distracted. Pick any instrumental music or meditational music which are known to be quite relaxing. Sounds have a specific effect on our brain. They have the power to stimulate relaxation chemicals or brainpower chemicals, all depending on what you hear.

When you feel as if you are ready to start your Reiki self-treatment, change into some comfortable loose clothes, go to your desired space where you will be performing the treatment, turn on your music for further relaxation, and take off your shoes and socks. Many practitioners and receivers can't relax with shoes and socks on. If you decide to lay down, place one pillow underneath your head while placing another pillow, rolled-up preferably, under your knees. If you'd like, you can also place a blanket on top of you for comfort and warmth throughout the treatment.

When balancing a specific element, you must first look at what particular space they are associated with. Since in this practice, we are focusing on water, this element is associated with ponds, rivers, oceans, and waterfalls. It will be easier for you to go to any of those destinations in order to achieve a balance within the water element. But you can also choose to stay at home. There is water within you; in fact, seventy percent of the body is made out of water. You should also consider taking a bowl or cup of water and placing it beside you if you are lying down or in front of you if you are sitting up. You should also consider doing this treatment after you've gone for a swim or taken a shower when your hair is wet, it will bring better results.

Start off by drinking some water before filling up the cup or bowl with water, preferably river or ocean water, but tap will do fine. Get yourself comfortable, either sitting up or lying down. Begin to close your eyes slowly, as if you are falling asleep. Take a deep breath in, hold it for a second or two before exhaling it slowly, pulling it for a second or two. Continue to breathe deeply for a couple of minutes, try to relax your body the best that you can. Get into the habit of deep breathing. Make a mental reminder through this treatment that Reiki is being used for the greater and higher good. If your mind and thoughts slip away during the breathing exercise, simply draw the attention back to the way your chest rises and falls or the way you breathe in and out.

Somewhere in the middle of your breathing exercise, say your Reiki prayer in your head or out loud if you wish. Ask to channel the Reiki energy, ask for guidance throughout the treatment, ask for the Reiki energy to resurface within your body, and set your intentions to heal the water element within your body and your mind. Call out to the element of water, ask it to help guide you through this session. At this point, you can also choose to use the symbols that you've learned in the previous chapter.

You can use the Power symbol and then the Mental/Emotional symbol by calling out their names three times and visualizing their symbol in your head. Repeat the words Choku Rei (Cho-Koo-Ray), the Power symbol, call out the name three times. Take some time to visualize the symbol in your head or draw it in the air in front of you. Set the right intention for the Power symbol, such as asking to enhance the energy and power of this treatment. Then repeat the words Sei He Ki (Say-Hay-Key), the Mental/Emotional symbol, call out the name three times. Take some time to visualize the symbol in your head or draw it in the air in front of you, besides the Power symbol. Set the right intention for the Mental/Emotional symbol such as asking to heal and balance the water element which represents your mind.

Go back to breathing deeply; make sure your mind is clear while you focus on breathing. After a couple of minutes of the breathing exercise, begin to visualize a lake, the ocean, or the pond. Take in the many details of your scenery. If you are physically present at that destination, then listen to the water but still make sure to visualize it in your head making you feel as if your eyes are open. The Heart and the Sacral chakras are mainly related to this treatment, but you can choose to give Reiki to all the other chakras since the water element is spread through your body within your veins.

If the lake or whatever place you are visualizing, imagine it as the core of the water element. Think of this water element and this big and round pond. Imagine yourself walking towards it, and carefully going in until the water is up to your waist. Visualize your body falling back, floating on the water, and feeling as light as a feather. Think of all your emotions coming in tune with the water. This water is balanced while your emotions and the water within you is not, so let the balanced water surround your body as you take a deep breathe in. Feel tingling sensations all throughout your body as both the energy radiating from you and the balanced water come in touch. Visualize the positive energy filling your entire body; you are swimming in a pond of positivity and emotional balance. It's so overwhelming that it influences the imbalance within your mind.

Imagine your anxiety fading into the water; let the water suck out all of your negative emotions, fears, and doubts. Let this water cleanse your whole being. All the negative feelings are replacing with the flow of Reiki energy, now that the negativity is gone, you are able to feel the flow of Reiki more precisely as more of the negative emotions leave your body. The water is encouraging the pure energy flow and guides it to your most tense area, which is the mind. Visualize all the negativity leaving your body, replacing it with emotional balance and the feelings of love, gratitude, self-care, and everything that is good and positive.

Encourage the flow of Reiki throughout your entire body and concentrate on the areas of the Heart chakra, which is located in your heart, and the Sacral chakra, which is located in your lower abdomen, a couple of inches below your belly button. Imagine the feelings of happiness, joy, pleasure, satisfaction, self-respect, love, and abundance fill you up until you become part of the pure water and this pure energy. Feel the Reiki healing your Heart and Sacral chakras, expanding the love capacity and the feelings of safety. The water within you has turned into pure and light energy, intertwining with the water around you.

When you feel as if you have visualized enough and that your mind is healed and any anxiety or negative emotions are all in the past, then you can begin by closing the treatment. Thank the universe or the Higher beings for their guidance. Thank the symbols for helping you balance your emotions and give more power to the treatment. Thank the element of water for being present, helping you through this process, and providing you with a lot of water to drink and use. Thank the Reiki healing energy for being able to give you the power to heal your emotional imbalance.

Finally, open your eyes and breathe normally. Take a minute or two to reflect on the treatment and notice any sensations throughout your body. Compare how you felt at the beginning of the session and at the end of the session. Drink the water that you have left in front of or beside you.

Full Physical Body Reiki Healing Meditation

Make sure to get rid of any distractions beforehand. Start off sitting upon the sacred place of your choosing. Your arms should lay right by your sides with the palms on your knees and facing upwards.

Take a deep breath in a while setting an intention for your body to relax. Slowly and gently, close your eyes and start breathing deeply. Inhale and hold the breath for a second and exhale, pulling the breath for another second. This breathing exercise ensures that your body will relax and it also provides you a focus point on something other than your thoughts. Think of nothing, meaning let your mind clear and empty itself as it brings focus on the way your chest rises and falls with each breath you take. If you find your mind drifting away and thinking about something, bring your attention back to the breathing by either paying attention to every time you inhale or exhale or simply to the way the chest rises and falls.

Activate the Power symbol, Choku Rei, by visualizing it hovering right in front of you. Hold the image for a minute while breathing deeply. Since this meditation will be focusing on giving healing to your whole body, you will also need to envision the Master symbol, Dai Ko Myo. Visualize the image of the symbol and hold it in your vision.

In your head, call out to the Universe or the Higher being and ask for guidance. Ask to channel the Reiki energy to be able to heal yourself effectively. Make an intention to help and heal the body and restore it to its natural flow of energy. If you'd like, you can form the Gassho hand position while asking the Universe for guidance.

Allow for the Reiki healing energy to resurface your body, glowing a bright white bulb of light as it takes a form all around your body. Imagine your Reiki resurfacing all throughout your body, channeling its energy. Let the Reiki energy be harnessed before setting an intention to center it on the palms of your hand. Imagine and focus on all of the Reiki energy being absorbed by the palms, forming a bright bulb of light.

Take a deep breath and begin by hovering your hands in front of your head. You will feel a strong pull towards the areas that will require your healing once you access the Reiki healing energy. Allow for your own auric field to guide you and pull your hands to where you need healing the most as you complete a quick body scan, that involves you hovering both of your hands from the head and making your way to the bottom to your feet, scanning the body in all areas. You will feel some tension, tingling, or a pull towards certain areas within the body.

Follow your intuition when doing a body scan, take a mental note of any areas that you can feel the tension in. Once you reach the end of the body where the feet are, make your way back up towards the head, double-checking if you missed any tension spots. Begin at the top where the head is, hover your hands in the air and imagine the Reiki light reemerging from within your hands and healing that area. Hover the hands in front of your head, do not make any skin-to-skin contact. Let the energy sink in as you slowly move your hands around the area, covering and hovering over each part of the head. From the very crown of the head to the sides and the temples. Make sure to cover all the ground. Allow for your hands to hover for at least thirty seconds before moving on, making its way down to the cheeks, the third eye region, the chin, and the rest of the face.

When you come across the area that possesses tension or something that pulls you in or away from it, then make physical contact with that part of the body. Place your hands on top of that tension, imagine the Reiki healing energy entering deeper and healing that area, releasing any tension, and encouraging the proper flow of Ki. Keep your hands on that area for about two to three minutes to ensure that it is healing before moving on.

Take your time as you move from place to place, once you pass the head, allow for your hands to hover around the throat region, making their way down to the shoulders. When it comes to your arms, use the opposite hand that is getting healed while hovering it over each of the arms. Allow for your hands to hover over your chest, stomach, lower abdomen, making their way to your legs, knees, and finally to your feet. You should spend at least thirty seconds hovering over each area, slowly moving around and making their way down to the bottom of the body.

Once you reach the feet, allow for the process to repeat again, but this time, let your hands travel from the feet all the way up to the crown of the chakra, covering and hovering over the tensed areas that you discovered during your quick body scan. Allow your hands to rest on those areas, making skin-to-skin contact for at least two to three minutes before moving on. Imagine cleansing the mind, healing from physical or mental trauma, lifting any tensions, purifying negative feelings, and healing the body.

Once your hands reach the crown, allow them to turn to the back of the body, which might be challenging to cover. Hold your hands over the back of the head, making their way to the back of the neck, the upper back, the lower back, the lower abdomen, and all the way to your feet. Rest your hands at the bottom before repeating the process and moving back to the top of the head while breathing in deeply.

Once you've finished with cleansing the mind, lift your hands up and form a Gassho position. Focus on the Completion symbol, Raku, and visualize the symbol in your head in order to activate it. Set an intention to seal the Reiki healing energy within your body. Thank the Universe or the Higher being for guidance and thank the Reiki energy for being able to give you the power to heal the receiver. Return the Reiki energy and spread it evenly around your body by visualizing your body glowing white before letting that white energy sunk inside.

Take a minute to casually rest and meditate normally, giving some time for the energy to sink in and for your body to heal. Once you are ready, gently open your eyes and lay down. Simply look up while taking another brief minute to reflect on your healing, take in on what you have experienced while the Reiki energy heals your body. Throughout the day, do not push yourself but rather take a break and give some time for your body to heal.

Chapter 8: Healing Others With Reiki

Reiki is such a powerful healing energy that it can be used to heal other people, your family, your friends, or even strangers. The best method of healing others using Reiki is through hands-on healing, which not only can be used when healing others, but when healing yourself too!

The hands-on healing is when you are making physical contact or hovering your hands above the person in certain parts of the body. The below image is a different hand position for hands-on healing for both yourself and others.

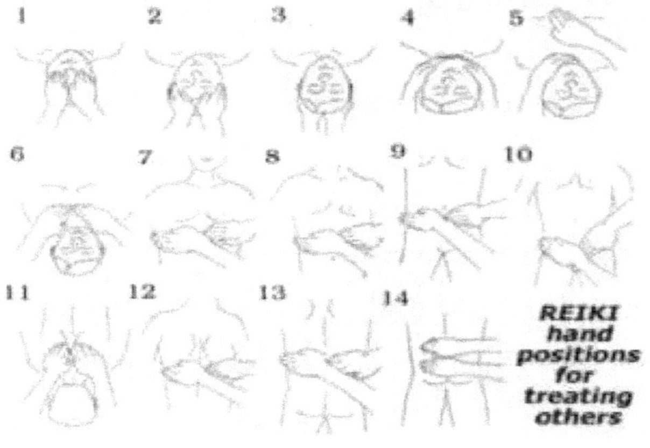

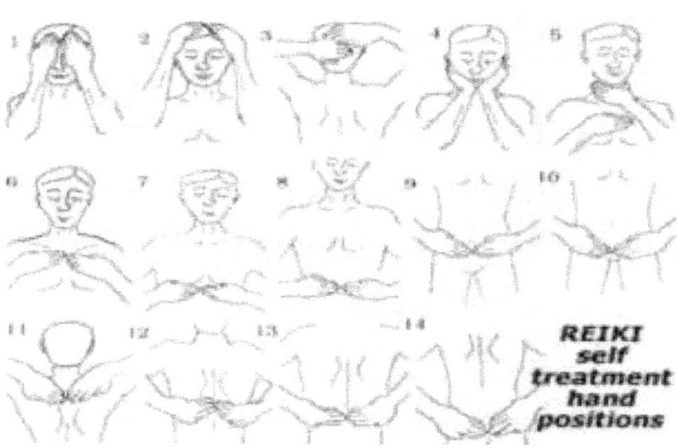

Before starting the hands-on healing, you should determine what exactly are you healing. If you are trying to get rid of back tension or pain, then you would place your hands on the back area, or where the pain resigns. If you are trying to get rid of anxiety, then you will place your hands around the head such as the numbers 1, 2, and 3 on both of the diagrams for treating others and yourself. Anxiety is also often linked to the Heart and the Sacral chakra in which you would use numbers 7 and 9 on both of the diagrams for treating yourself and others. When healing the body as a whole or just practicing Reiki healing on others, you would start off with our hands hovering over the receivers head with the intention of the Universe or the Higher being to guide your hands to the place where requires the most healing.

When healing one's mind with Reiki energy and using the hands-on technique, there are a couple of things the practitioner, which is you, should be aware of. You should be familiar with performing Reiki on yourself before jumping into performing Reiki for others. You need to be on Reiki II and receive the Reiki II attunement in order to be able to heal others and send distance healing.

Full-body Reiki Healing

This healing technique is about healing the receiver's body and where most of the tension is located. When healing others with Reiki, you should first communicate with them beforehand. The receiver should come to you prepared. It's the same concept when you are performing Reiki healing on yourself. Both the practitioner and the receiver should wear comfortable and loose clothes, with no jewelry. Both the practitioner and the receiver should drink one glass of water before the treatment.

Start off by making the receiver lay down on a bed or couch. Place a pillow underneath their head and another pillow, rolled up preferably, underneath your knees. Tell the receiver to relax, close their eyes, and start breathing deeply. Inhale and hold the breath for a second and exhale, pulling the breath for another second. This breathing exercise ensures that the receiver's body will relax, and it also provides them to focus on something. Tell the receiver to think of nothing, meaning let their minds clear and empty themselves as they focus on the way their chest rises and falls. If they find their mind drifting away and thinking about something, let them know that it is okay and remind them to just bring the attention back to the breathing.

Take a deep breath and begin by hovering your hand in front of the receivers head. Close your eyes for a minute to concentrate. Take a deep breath in and out to relax your body and clear your mind. In your head, call out to the Universe or the Higher being and ask for guidance. Ask to channel the Reiki energy to be able to heal the person in front of you. Make an intention to help and heal the receiver. If you'd like, you can form the Gassho hand position while asking the Universe for guidance. Imagine your Reiki resurfacing all throughout your body, channel the energy, and concentrate on centering it inside your hands. Imagine your body glowing and that glow moving towards the palm of your hands. Visualize the palms of your hands glowing and filling up with white and pure light.

Proceed to open your eyes and imagine the light joining with the aura of the receiver. You will feel a strong pull towards the areas that will require healing, so let the aura of the receiver and your Reiki energy guide your hands. If you can't feel any pull, then simply do a body scan meaning hover both of your hands from the head of the receiver and to their feet. You will feel some tension or pull towards certain areas in their body. Often there is more than one. You will be required to follow your intuition, which is why it was mentioned earlier that you should practice Reiki self-healing because it can help increase one's intuition skills.

Follow your intuition when doing a body scan, take a mental note of any areas that you can feel the tension in. Once you reach the end of the body where the feet are, make your way back up towards the head, double-checking if you missed any tension spots. Begin at the top where the head is, hover your hands in the air and imagine the Reiki light reemerging and healing the patient. You will be using the diagram above for guidance, start off on number 1. You can skip number 3 because it is easier to do when the receiver is laying on their stomach, which will happen later in the session. When hovering the hands above the receiver in the places that don't have tension, you would only stay anywhere from thirty seconds to one minute to ensure that area is purified and the Reiki is flowing through there. Make your way to the side of the head, then the bottom, then the chins, and etc. following the diagram above.

When you come across the area that possesses tension or something that pulls you in or away from it, then make physical contact with the receiver. Place your hands on top of that tension and close your eyes, imagine the Reiki healing energy entering the receiver and healing that area, releasing any tension, and encouraging the flow of Ki. Keep your hands on that area for about two to three minutes to ensure that it is healing before moving on. When you reach number 10 on the diagram, you will no longer have to hover your hands for thirty seconds, instead slowly proceed to the end of the body, where the feet are. If you feel any tension, then proceed by placing your hands on the area, focusing and healing, for about two to three minutes before moving on.

Ask the receiver to then turn around, laying on their stomach with their back facing up. Proceed to hover your hands in the hair around the head area. This time you can finally do number 3 before proceeding to 11, 12, etc. Make your way slowly keeping at least thirty seconds on each spot before moving on. Remember where you felt tension when the receiver was facing up? You are going to place your hands on the exact spot but this time on the other side of the body. Keep your hands on the spot for about two to three minutes before moving on. You are doing the exact same thing you did when the receiver was facing up.

When you are done and have reached the feet of the receiver, let them know that it's time to turn back around. Place your hands on their head, number 1, and making physical contact. Close your eyes and focus on clearing the mental and emotional area. If the receiver is uncomfortable with you placing your hands on their face, then you can just hover in the air. You have purified the body and now take some time to purify the mind, which is the control system of the body. Hold your hands there for two to three minutes. Imagine cleansing the mind, lifting any tensions and negative feelings that can affect the body too.

Once you've finished with cleansing the mind, lift your hands up and form a Gassho position. Close your eyes and focus on the Power symbol. Repeat Choku Rei (Cho-Koo-Ray) about three times before visualizing the symbol in your head in order to activate it. Set an intention to seal the Reiki healing energy within the client to ensure that the healing energy will still work its magic even when you are not around. Thank the Universe or the Higher being for guidance and thank the Reiki energy for being able to give you the power to heal the receiver. Open your eyes and tell the receiver to open their eyes. You can let the receiver lay and rest for a moment to reflect and take in whatever it is that they might feel within their body before dismissing them.

However, you are not finished. Once the receiver has left the room, you have to clear the energy that you picked up when healing the receiver. Often time when you are giving Reiki, some of this energy returns back to you who is the vessel. And many times, the energy does not come alone. A lot of people have very negative energies attached to them, although Reiki can help clear them all, you should also clear the negative energies too just in case if they attached themselves to you.

To make sure that it doesn't happen, take a seat and close your eyes. Call out to the Completion symbol, which is responsible for banishing any negative energies that you might have picked up from the receiver. Repeat the words Raku (Ra-Koo) three times or how many times you think is necessary. Imagine the symbol floating in the air and direct your attention to cleansing your body and healing energy. Resurface your Reiki energy and take a deep breath. Let the Reiki flow through your body with the intent of purifying it. Take some time to sit in quiet and experience the Reiki energy flowing through you. When done, simply thank the symbol for the help and thank the Reiki energy for purifying your body.

You can also heal a person who is not physically present to you, with the help from the Distance healing symbol. There are many techniques that can help you smoothen this process and make sure the Reiki energy reaches the receiver.

Reiki Through A Photograph

You are always welcome to use a photograph to focus on the person who will be receiving the Reiki energy. You can ask the patient or whoever you are sending Reiki to, to give you their photograph to send Reiki through them. If you only have the name and the location, it will work but not as efficiently as knowing exactly who you are giving Reiki energy to. Make sure that the receiver is aware that this healing is being done on them since they will be able to feel it. It will be better if you schedule a specific time so the receiver will lay down and relax during the process, or take a nap. This technique can also be used on those who are not aware that Reiki is being done on them; they will still be able to feel it.

For this method, you will need a picture and a marker. Place the picture in front of you, close your eyes, and ask the Universe for guidance. Call on your Reiki healing energy and concentrate to center this energy on your hands. Breathe deeply for a few minutes before opening your eyes and picking up the pen or marker that you've placed next to the picture. Turn the picture around and draw the Power symbol and the Distance symbol. If the receiver has a specific problem it hand, think if the Master symbol or the Mental/Emotional symbol should be used. If the receiver has a specific problem that they need help with, then write the problem down on a piece of paper along with the symbols but slightly changing the intention of the symbol to helping the receiver with the problem instead of sending healing.

Write down the Power symbol first. Say the words Choku Rei (Cho-Koo-Ray) three times before proceeding with writing the Distance symbol. Say the words Hon Sha Ze ShoNen (Hon-Sha-Zee-Show-Nen) three times before picking up the paper and holding it in your hands. Form a Gassho with your hands and place the photograph in between your palms. Close your eyes and imagine the symbols, each for at least thirty seconds to sixty seconds. Let your Reiki energy join in with the intentions and the symbols of the photograph. Visualize the healing energy shining white and pure color. Lift your hands up, still in the Gassho position with the image between palms Imagine that energy is a white shining ball which leaves your hand and flying up into the Universe and towards the person that is waiting to receive it on the other side.

To finish off, thank the Universe, the symbols, and the Reiki healing energy for helping you. You can keep the image and practice sending Reiki a couple of times per week until the problem or discomfort of the receiver goes away.

Using An Object

You can use an object, a stuffed toy, or a surrogate of any kind instead of a picture. If the person is close to you and you know their name and how they look like then mentally imagine that this object or toy is the person. Just like when using the photograph, make sure that the receiver is aware that the Reiki energy is being transferred to them for a more effective and smooth transition.

Proceed by asking for guidance, imagining, and saying out loud the symbols for the Power symbol and the Distance symbol. Concentrate on resurfacing the Reiki healing energy, before picking up the object or toy. If you'd like, you can form a Gassho and place the toy in between your hands. Imagine the light entering the object or the body of the stuffed toy. Visualize and put intention for healing the receiver's body. You can even perform the full-body Reiki healing if it's a stuffed animal. Since the receiver is not physically present with you, you do not need to use the Completion symbol.

When using an object to heal a person's mental and emotional state, visualize this object to be the mind of the receiver. Hold it with both your hands and direct the Reiki healing power there with the Mental/Emotional symbol. You can even find a small rock outside in nature and use it to represent the person. Using a marker to write the purpose for this healing on one side and any corresponding symbols on the other side. Since the rock is small, it can be held in between two hands. You can direct your Reiki energy into the object, sealing it at the end with the Power symbol. This object can also be given to the receiver to keep on them at all times. It can be used in situations to give one good luck for a certain event that will happen in the future or simply give healing.

Reiki Through The Third Eye

If you can see the person in your line of sight, but you can't physically perform the Reiki, you can always use your third eye to help you. If your third eye is open, then you will be able to use this technique easily. Allow your Reiki to emerge and flow through your body. Concentrate and center the energy where your third eye is located, in the middle of your forehead slightly above the middle of your brows. Focus and gather your Reiki healing energy there. Imagine a beam of light coming from your third eye and connecting with the receiver's third eye with the intention to heal. You can even draw symbols with the beam of light to strengthen the Reiki healing energy. This technique can also be used over a photo or simply imagining that the person is standing in front of you.

Simple Imagination

Like briefly mentioned earlier, your imagination is a powerful tool when it comes to Reiki. When performing the Reiki healing on a person who is not physically present with you, you can use your imagination to visualize the person standing right in front of you or image the person inside your palms as you keep them cupped up together.

Begin to breathe in deeply for a few minutes before asking the Universe for guidance and resurfacing your Reiki energy. Say the Distance symbol and any other symbols relating to the treatment. Proceed by visualizing the person receiving Reiki, if you are using the cupped on your hand's method then simply imagine them receiving the Reiki energy and swimming in it. If you visualize the person standing in front of you, then lift your hands and imagine a white and pure Reiki light emerging from your hands and traveling to the person in front of you with the intention to heal that person.

Imagine them feeling better and returning to their previous and healthy state. You can also keep on imagining the Distance symbol or any other symbols used throughout your Reiki practice to ensure that the person is receiving the Reiki. When you have finished, do not forget to thank the Universe for guidance and for the power and the help of the symbols.

Intention Box

Another great technique is to have an intention box that you will with rolled up papers with intentions. This technique is good for when you are giving Reiki to a lot of people, for example, emotional and mental healing after a traumatic event, Reiki can be given at the same time to all the people involved.

Make sure that you are sitting down, with your legs crossed. Place your hands in a mudra position, with the palms facing up. Begin by taking a deep breath in, hold it in for a two to three seconds before exhaling. Concentrate on resurfacing your Reiki energy and center it in both of your palms. This should take a couple of minutes.

Open your eyes and pick up a small piece of paper and a pen or marker. Begin by writing your intention on the paper, what is it that you want to send through Reiki? Healing emotionally, headlining physically, or healing mentally? You can write down any intentions that you want but avoid using words such as no, can't, won't, not, don't, etc. Avoid any hint of negativity inside your intentions. Also, do not use periods, the full stops. After writing the intention, add the following:

'Thank you Reiki, Thy will be done, It is so.'

Turn the paper around and write any symbols relating to your intention. You must include the Distance symbol, for it is necessary when performing distance healing. Roll the paper up or fold it however you want. Make a Gassho hand position and place the paper in between your palms. Visualize the light and Reiki emerging from your fingers and your palms and sinking into the paper. Stay in this sensation for at least one to two minutes before placing the paper inside the box.

You can always put more than one intention inside the box, for example, 'I send my Reiki healing energy to [Last Name] family to experience emotional healing' and 'I send my Reiki energy to make sure that the [First Name] [Last Name] will receive blessing and security in the future.' You can write as many intentions as you want and direct them to how many people you want. Keep in mind which symbols that you use.

Once you have written all the intentions, rolled the papers up, transferred Reiki into them, and placed them inside the box. Hold the box in between your hands and focus on transferring more Reiki energy into the box. Visualize the new energy swimming inside the box and visualize the symbols that you have used, you can even call out their name if it's easier for you to focus. LIft the box up in the air, right above your head, and focus on giving that Reiki energy one last push. Imagine that energy shooting up into the sky all out once, each traveling to different people, places, or events.

You can continue to add more intentions throughout the week, but make sure to activate their symbols and their Reiki energy by visualizing them and releasing them into the Universe. This ensures that all the people or places will receive their Reiki healing.

Conclusion

Thank you for making it through to the end of *Reiki Healing for Beginners: The Ultimate Guide to Reiki Meditation and Reiki Healing to Increase Your Energy and Defeat the Daily Anxiety,* let's hope it was informative and able to provide you with all the tools you need to achieve your goals of healing yourself and others.

The next step is to put everything that you have learned to the test by attuning yourself to Reiki and practicing healing yourself before moving on and healing others. You have all the tools you need to live a healthy and free life of any illnesses and problems. Use the power of Reiki to help yourself, your family, your friends, and others around you. Not only can Reiki heal, but it also send you on a spiritual journey full of self-discovery, and it can push you to your life path.

Finally, if you find this book useful in any way, a review on Amazon is always appreciated!

Description

If you ever wanted to have the ability to heal yourself and others around you, then keep reading! How would you react if you found out it is possible? And not only that, but you can also use Reiki to influence different events in the future and the past, get rid of feelings of anxiety or other mental issues as well as healing your own physical body!

When it comes to Reiki, there is no such thing as time and distance. Reiki healing energy can reach anything, anytime, and anywhere. With the information and guidance in this book, you will be able to learn how to access this majestic Universal energy known as Reiki. The book, *Reiki Healing for Beginners,* contains everything that you need to know about Reiki, how to access it, how to self-attune yourself, and how to practice the art of healing yourself and others around you!

Reiki is a healing energy that is able to heal any physical problems within the body, as well as the mental problems within the mind, such as anxiety, depression, and negative thinking, which play an important role in the body's health.

This book will point you in the right direction when it comes to spiritual growth, personal growth, and your life path. Many practitioners and Reiki Masters are able to use Reiki to their benefit, and so can you! This book is for anyone, beginners, practitioners, and even Reiki Masters can benefit from learning various techniques that are only here to help. In this book, you will learn about the following:

- Origins of Reiki energy
- Various methods and techniques for healing others
- Different types of Reiki levels, symbols, and systems
- How to heal yourself, others, and even animals
- What will one experience during a Reiki attunement
- How energy within the body affects the health
- And many more!

Relaxation and Stress Reduction for Beginners

A Mindfulness-Based Program

Robin McGill

Furthermore, the information that can be found within the pages described forthwith shall be considered both accurate and truthful when it comes to the recounting of facts. As such, any use, correct or incorrect, of the provided information will render the Publisher free of responsibility as to the actions taken outside of their direct purview. Regardless, there are zero scenarios where the original author or the Publisher can be deemed liable in any fashion for any damages or hardships that may result from any of the information discussed herein.

Additionally, the information in the following pages is intended only for informational purposes and should thus be thought of as universal. As befitting its nature, it is presented without assurance regarding its prolonged validity or interim quality. Trademarks that are mentioned are done without written consent and can in no way be considered an endorsement from the trademark holder.

Introduction

Congratulations on purchasing this book, and thank you for doing so. This book will help you in understanding stress and the ways to bring it down.

The stress levels in society are increasing alarmingly. A study conducted by the American Psychological Association (APA) found that the general stress levels rose from 4.9 to 5.1 on a scale of 1-10. This may just look like an increase of two points, but accounting for society as a whole the number is big as the healthy score should be around 3.8. In a survey, around 44% of adults reported their stress levels had increased a lot in the past 5 years.

This is something that can be felt even without conducting such detailed surveys. People are feeling more and more stressed. Most people find themselves crumbling under stress at the workplace and home. They find it difficult to handle the stress, and it is affecting their productivity as well as personal lives.

Despite so many studies and widespread awareness about stress, nothing much is happening. More and more people are coming under its paws, and people already battling with it are feeling the pressure with greater intensity. This shows that something is wrong deep within.

Stress is a very complex issue, and it affects us on various levels. When trying to deal with the stress, we generally look for quick fixes and instant relaxation, and this means that the real reasons remain unaddressed. This is the main reason that no real change is taking place.

Stress not only affects us emotionally and mentally, but it also affects us physiologically. If we do the symptomatic treatment, the root cause of the stress will remain as it is, and hence, there would be no actual relief.

This book has tried to explore stress in detail for you. It will help you in understanding stress in detail. You would be able to understand the various levels on which stress affects us and the underlying causes.

For your ease of understanding, this book has tried to classified stress into various categories so that you can identify your stressors properly and look for definitive treatment.

This book has been divided into three main parts:

The first part of the book will try to explain stress in detail. It will subdivide stress into various categories so that you can understand the kind of stress that might be affecting you. You will be able to see the impact it has on your body, mind, and behavior. You will also get to know the major causes of stress so that you can look for them around you clearly.

The second part will help you in dealing with mental stress, stress at your workplace, and home. It will give you definitive tips to deal with stress in various spheres. All the aspects of stress management have been covered in this part in great detail.

The third and the final part will bring to you various techniques that can be used in day to day life to lower stress and induce relaxation. This part doesn't limit itself to simply defining the techniques but gives you real examples to deal with stress. From deep breathing exercises, meditation script to visualization, everything has been given to you for better understanding and use.

This book is a sincere attempt to help you in dealing with stress. It is an attempt to cover the topic above and beyond definitions. It will help you in dealing with stress in real life.

The tips and tricks are practical and can be employed as you read the book. The purpose is to enable you to deal with the menace of stress in real life.

Every effort has been made to ensure that this book delivers complete and comprehensive information about meditation to you. I hope that you will find it highly informative and useful.

There are plenty of books on this subject on the market, thanks again for choosing this one! Every effort was made to ensure it is full of as much useful information as possible. Please enjoy it!

Chapter 1: Understanding Stress

What is Stress?

I thought of beginning this book with something poetic or inspiring. Something that would help you in having a positive outlook towards the whole idea of stress. Positivity works wonders in dealing with stress, and that's something I plan to do in the whole book. However, I believe not beginning the book with some core problems would be an injustice.

People keep pushing others to deal with stress playfully. They want you to ignore stress and move on.

Stress isn't something with which you play. You deal with it.

Stress isn't something that you ignore. It needs to be acknowledged and addressed.

The whole concept of stress is highly misunderstood. It has been painted as a villain — the cause of most of the problems we are facing today. There is no doubt that stress has an important role to play in our miseries, but it is a result and not the cause of the problem. Blaming stress for the problems is like putting the cart before horses.

Stress is a highly generalized term these days. It is used as an umbrella term for anything that feels inconvenient or maybe unpleasant. However, stress originates when things start to happen over which you have little or no control.

This is very important to note. The main cause of stress is things getting out of your control or plan.

If you pay close attention, in a single day, dozens of such things happen.

Does that mean all such things cause stress?

Yes.

However, every kind of stress is not bad. The stress of all types doesn't need to be your concern.

Your body is well equipped to deal with stress to a great extent. In fact, some stress is even good for the body. It makes you quick and responsive.

Stress triggers several biological processes in the body. These processes play a very important role in the secretion of various chemicals and hormones in your body. In crucial moments of threat, these chemicals and hormones can play a very important role in your survival.

Stress can also work as a motivator. Some people may even find it thrilling to live through stressful moments as it gives them the adrenaline rush.

In dangerous situations, stress can be a lifesaver. It helps you in staying awake. It keeps your responses on-point. You even get some superhuman reflexes.

However, it's all well and good when such stressful situations are few and far between.

Stress is a non-physical response to situations that are beyond your control, and it can lead to biological and chemical responses.

It is similar to inflammation to a great extent.

When your body gets attacked in any manner, it starts an inflammatory response. The immune system goes into overdrive and starts the damage control work. Imagine that attack being very big or very long. It would lead to chronic inflammation, and the very inflammatory system that was designed to protect you starts working against you.

The same thing happens with stress.

The human body is designed to bear some level of stress. However, when stress becomes a norm, or you stop addressing the main cause of the stress, the problem becomes serious.

This book will help you in understanding stress in detail.

- It will explain the way in which stress work.
- The chemical and biological processes involved during stress and the impact they have on your body.

- The main causes of stress
- Their physical, mental, emotional, and behavioral effect on your life
- The ways to react to stress and overcome it
- Simple ways of identifying changeable and unchangeable stressors
- Inculcating positive habits at the workplace and home that can help in lowering stress
- Powerful techniques that can really help to bring stress down

Pathology of Stress

The body response is generated when your mind senses danger or a situation that is beyond control. In the physical term, this means that you are in a situation from which fighting or getting out immediately is required. In psychological or emotional terms, it can be a situation in which you find yourself in a trap from which wriggling out seems to be difficult, and you aren't well prepared.

In such situations, the hypothalamus at the base of your brain starts to react. It directs the adrenal glands to release to important hormones called the adrenaline and cortisol. Both these hormones are very powerful and can power you up.

- **Increases the Heartbeat:** This means your heart starts pumping more blood. The muscles in your body start getting more oxygenated blood, and hence, it becomes easier for them to work better.

- **Rapid Breathing:** This also helps your body in inhaling more oxygen. To get into a turbo power mode, your body needs a lot of oxygen, and for that, the breathing rate goes up tremendously in stressful situations.

- **Glycogen Stored in Muscles is Put to Use:** The body stores glucose in the form of glycogen in muscles for contingency measures. It is these kinds of situations that those glycogen stores are used. When you are stressed, facing danger, or need fast reflexes, all the muscles in your body need to work perfectly. This process gives your body the required ability. Your muscles start getting an ample amount of oxygen to use the glycogen store, and every muscle becomes powerful all of a sudden.

- **Contraction of Blood Vessels:** The blood vessels get contracted to that more, and more blood can be directed to the muscles. The complete focus of the body in such situations is to provide the right fight or flight response. All this is happening to either facilitate rapid escape or formidable defense.

- **Insulin Production Comes to a Halt:** A major function of the insulin in the body is to lower the glucose levels in the body. However, glucose is the main power source, and when caught in a dire situation, the power reserve is crucial, and hence, the production of insulin stops. It is done to conserve every bit of fuel reserve available. The more glucose you have, the longer you would be able to fight or run.

The Cortisol Hormone

- **Raises Glucose Levels:** You need all the glucose that your body can get, and the cortisol hormone is all for it. As the cortisol levels rise, the glucose levels in your bloodstream start to rise as it starts knocking at all sources. In normal circumstances, the body tries its best to lower the blood glucose levels as fast as possible. However, in stressful situations, things start working in a completely opposite direction. Glucose becomes a prized commodity.

- **Ensures Effective Glucose Supply to the Brain:** The brain is a big consumer of glucose. It needs a lot of glucose to run all its processes. When in stressful situations, the demand goes up even more. The cortisol hormone ensures that the uninterrupted supply of glucose is maintained in such situations. This is a reason people start thinking so fast in stressful situations. They are able to pay great attention to every detail and hear things clearly. Time seems to start running slowly for them. It all happens because their brain is working extra fast while the time is running at its usual pace.

- **Stops Non-Essential Functions:** All the functions that are not a part of the survival plan are brought to a standstill. The body starts conserving energy to the last bit.

- **Parts of Brain Controlling Motivation, Fear, and Mood:** Your brain has a specialized area that deals with such emotions. Logic or reason is usually in the driving seat, however, when caught in stressful situations, fear, motivation, and mood can work better, and that's what happens. The brain gives the command to an area dominated by these instincts.

Adrenaline isn't primarily a stress hormone. It is a hormone that leads to a fight or flight response. Cortisol is a stress hormone. It puts your body in survival mode and begins all the responses that might be needed to save you at the moment. Both hormones work in conjunction.

However, all this has a cost. You will feel burned out as soon as you get out of danger or stress.

Now, if you find yourself caught in stressful situations once in a while, your body is most likely to get over it. I used most likely because even acute stress, when faced in severe circumstances, can lead to serious dissociative symptoms like *Post Traumatic Stress Disorders* (PTSD)

Stress has developed as a form of evolutionary advantage. It gives you an edge over predators and helps you survive. However, putting the body into turbo power mode has its costs. When your brain senses danger, it pumps the Corticotropin-Releasing Hormones (CRH). These hormones are responsible for the production of adrenaline and cortisol. These hormones can take a toll on your body. They pump you up, but prolonged exposure to these hormones can be dangerous for your body.

For instance, frequent adrenaline release can:

- **Harm Blood Vessels:** Abnormal contraction and expansion of blood vessels without proper preparation can be harmful to them. For instance, when you undertake intense physical exercise, your body releases nitric oxide, which makes your blood vessels flexible. But, adrenaline leads to the same thing without proper preparation, and hence, it can be harmful if that same thing starts happening repeatedly.

- **High Blood Pressure:** It can also lead to high blood pressure, which is a chronic condition and has serious implications for your health. It will start affecting several vital organs.

- **Headaches:** If there are frequent adrenaline surges, you may also start experiencing severe bouts of headaches, which can be a cause of the trouble.

- **Anxiety:** Anxiety is also a result of frequent adrenaline surge. You start developing a fear of the unknown. There is a heightened sense of perceived danger that might not even be real but would have the same detrimental effect on your body and health.

- **Sleep Disorders:** This is, again, a serious issue that comes with frequent adrenaline surges. People with this problem usually develop sleep disorders that may also lead to insomnia. Several factors, like fear and anxiety, are also working in the background to contribute to that.

- **Weight Gain:** Adrenaline hormone, if regulated properly, can help in rapid fat burning. However, when the adrenaline release goes uncontrolled and frequent, it can also lead to weight gain. The main stress hormone cortisol also has a key role to play in it.

Irregulated Cortisol Release also leads to similar issues. In fact, it accentuates the problems created by the frequent adrenaline surges.

- **Weight Gain:** Cortisol has a very important role to play in weight gain. It is the main hormone that starts meddling with your blood sugar levels and insulin release. When the cortisol levels in your blood start remaining high, all kinds of fat burning comes to a standstill. Your body is in a constant conservation mode, and hence any energy expenditure that should have taken place in normal circumstances stops. The constant state of stress causes fatigue, and you keep feeling tired. The normal functioning of the body also gets compromised. The result is weight gain. Have you noticed that people facing depression or high stress suddenly start gaining weight, although there is no dramatic change in their diet?

- **Feeling Energy Drained:** You may start feeling energy drained and unenthusiastic about everything. It is very natural to happen as your body cannot sustain being in a constant turbo power mode. Chronic stress simply puts your body out of balance. You just keep feeling energy drained and may not want to do anything at all.

- **Type 2 Diabetes:** This is a serious physiological problem that high cortisol presence can cause. When the cortisol levels in your body start remaining consistently high, they mess with the insulin sensitivity of your body. Your body starts maintaining a high blood sugar level but keeps feeling low in energy whereas, in normal circumstances, it should be the opposite. Insulin released by the pancreas is not able to bring down the blood sugar levels down effectively, and it begins the process of insulin resistance, which is a precursor to diabetes. Therefore, if the cortisol levels in your body start to remain high, unnatural weight gain and diabetes may come as physiological side effects besides other problems.

- **Brain Fog, Poor Memory, and Other Cognitive Issues:** Excessive stress and the presence of high levels of stress hormones also have a detrimental impact on cognitive function. It can lead to chronic inflammation in the brain that may cause neurodegenerative issues and may also reduce neuroplasticity. In simple words, the ability of the brain to keep renewing itself goes down. The stress will definitely take a toll on the brain.

- **Poor Immune System:** Like the brain, stress also pumps up the immune system. The charged-up immune system in times of distress is good, but if it remains on high alert all the time, it will lose its strength, and that's what happens if the cortisol levels remain consistently high in case of prolonged stress.

- **Other Problems like High Blood Pressure, Sleep Disorders, Anxiety, and Headaches Become Strong:** Consistently high levels of cortisol levels in the blood would give a push to all the problems that come with the adrenaline surge.

Why Do You Need to Know About Stress?

The purpose of this long explanation of the impact of stress is to clarify the way in which stress affects you physiologically. When people talk about stress, they are mainly talking about the mental and emotional impact of stress, and the physiological or biological part is completely left out.

If you want to deal with stress in the correct manner, it is important that you accept that stress is a very real thing that not only has mental and emotional ramifications but physical ones too.

Most people are never really able to get out of the vicious cycle of stress because they keep thinking it as a fancy term invented to define problems.

It is important that you understand that stress is a real thing.

- People suffering from chronic stress need help. They need to take steps to get out of the problem. However, chronic stress is the main branch people are concerned about.

- Overwhelming stress can prove to be even worse. If you have unfortunately been through some serious trauma or have lost someone dear, you may need help even more.

Stress isn't the cause of your problems. The stress is simply your body's reaction to an adverse situation or demand. Stress isn't something that happens to you. Stress is the manner in which you react to a stressful situation.

This means if your response is quick and you are able to get over a situation fast, there isn't much to worry about. Unfortunately, that doesn't happen very often. People get caught in the response. They keep reacting in abnormal ways for much longer than required, and that leads to chronic stress or react in an abnormal manner making it overwhelming stress. Most of the time, the person reacting is completely unaware of the response as the process is internal, and hence, getting help becomes even more difficult.

In the following parts, we will discuss the various types of stress we face and the effect they can have on us.

The 3 Types of Stress

On the basis of duration and frequency, the stress is divided into 3 main parts:

1. Acute Stress
2. Episodic Acute Stress
3. Chronic Stress

1. Acute Stress

We all experience acute stress in our day to day lives. It is a moment of rush that all of a sudden gives you the goosebumps.

- Imagine you are driving by leisurely, and suddenly, a car Zooms inches away from you.
- Your car is losing control, and you somehow regain control seconds before it is about to hit anything.
- You are doing something you shouldn't be doing, and you are caught off guard.

- The rush of blood flowing through your veins felt when you are taking a thrilling ride

Acute stress is generally immediate and intense. You suddenly feel the rush of blood briefly, and then everything returns to normal. This brief moment is enough to break sweats and invoke great clarity and alertness.

This kind of stress doesn't necessarily need to be in bad situations. For instance, people taking thrilling rides also feel acute stress, but they like it. Usually, the stress of this kind is brief and doesn't have a long-term impact on your physiology.

However, severe acute stress is an exception to this. People who experience severe acute stress in which either they encounter some really tough situations, view gory things, or face the loss of someone known and dear to them find it very difficult to recover. Such people may suffer from disassociative disorders and may even face PTSD. These people would need professional medical help.

Otherwise, acute stress is a part of our daily life. We don't keep such things in our long-term memory, and hence, they don't have a far-reaching mental or emotional impact.

2. Episodic Acute Stress

Episodic acute stress takes place when you start finding yourself in stressful situations more often than usual. People engaged in high-risk professions like fire-fighting, racing, counter-terrorism, rescue work, etc. may face the risk of this problem more often.

However, it would be incorrect to say that only people involved in high-risk jobs are vulnerable. People with irregular work habits, poor lifestyle, or chaotic life may also experience this.

For instance, if you have taken loans from too many people, and they can come knocking at your door any time, you may experience episodic acute stress. You may start living in the constant fear that someone may come knocking anytime. The knocking is not the problem. The real problem is the fear that someone may knock at any moment or may knock at the time when you are least expecting someone.

This may also happen to people who have poor work management. They also live in constant fear that they may be asked about work anytime. They are unable to finish the work in this fear.

This constant fear of the perceived danger is what does the biggest damage. The fear and anxiety are bad not only for your mental health but also for physical well-being as they are raising your stress levels. You always feel tense and alert. You are never really able to relax completely. Even when not in danger of being called out, your sensors are worried about the things that may happen in the future. This can take out peace and relaxation from life.

These are just a few examples. You can pick any of your fears and visualize yourself.

- People who are not punctual face this risk
- The people who unorganized in their personal and professional life
- People with poor interpersonal skills

This stress can be really damaging.

3. Chronic Stress

When people start experiencing high-stress levels all the time, they tend to suffer from chronic stress. The reasons for this kind of stress can be physiological, psychological, and environmental.

- A person who has lost a spouse may experience chronic stress
- People living in dysfunctional families may also experience the same
- An unhappy marriage or unemployment may also lead to chronic stress

However, if a person is suffering from some chronic illness that keeps that person in constant pain or fear of pain, that may also cause a significant amount of chronic stress.

People suffering from PTSD also have to endure chronic stress as they are not able to get over the incident, and it keeps playing in their mind over and over again.

If a person has the responsibility of another person who isn't getting any better and the care is taking up a lot of your time, money, and effort, that person is likely to suffer from chronic stress. This is irrespective of the feelings towards that person. The caregiver may be completely devoted to the care of that person. It is the fear and grief of the loss of time, money, and effort that leads to stress, and you may not have any way to control it effectively.

The severity of stress goes up as you move from episodic acute stress to chronic stress.

Emotional, Behavioral, and Physical Impact of Stress

Stress has a deep impact on a victim's life. As we already know, stress is our reaction to an adverse situation. The reactions may vary from person to person. This means two individuals may react to the same situation in a different way.

Some people may become very calm in stressful situations, while others may show a sign of panic. It all depends on the person's temperaments and the ability to handle stress. It'd be incorrect to term any specific reaction as normal. Our reactions to adverse situations are dependent on our perception of threat.

A person with a weak financial background may view the loss of a job as a catastrophe and may show a very sharp reaction. On the other hand, a person with a stable financial background, laid back attitude, or lack of responsibility in hindsight may not register it very aggressively. The situation remains the same, but the reactions change from person to person.

In the same manner, reaction to the loss of a loved one would also vary from person to person. Some people are able to bear the loss of a loved one stoically, while others may exhibit violent reactions. This is in no way a reflection of the manner in which the event is going to affect them in the long-term. In fact, some people who are able to vent out their remorse at the time of the incident are able to cope with the event better later on.

Stress affects our lives in more ways than one. Not only do we get affected mentally, but it also alters our behavior and physiology.

General Impact of stress can be divided into 3 main categories:

1. Emotional Impact
2. Behavioral Impact

3. Physiological Impact

Every individual may react in a different manner. However, there are some common signs that people exhibit. If you want to examine the way you react to stress on various levels, try to find the number of reactions you exhibit or have exhibited in the past.

1. Emotional Impact

Stress has a deep impact on our minds. In fact, stress is mainly caused due to perceived threat. It means the threat perception is largely in your mind. It is your mind that's making it big or small. Two people from the same financial background may take the news of the loss of the job very differently. It would vary on the way the news gets registered by their minds.

The impact of stress can be positive, as well as negative. Some people get motivated to do more in stressful situations, while others may simply feel fear struck. The important thing is to evaluate the kind of reaction you generally have without judgment. This would, later on, help in dealing with stress on various levels.

- **Anxiety:** It is generally the first, and one of the most common reactions people have to stress. We all feel anxious in stressful situations. Either the stress is positive or negative, anxiety is always there. Imagine yourself awaiting the news of a baby to be born or your name to called out in a draw of lots. The outcome in both situations is going to be positive, yet you feel anxious nonetheless. It is the same with negative scenarios. Anxiety is the first effect of stress. To an extent, anxiety is not alarming; however, if it goes out of hand, it can create problems on several levels that we will discuss later on and also the way to keep it low.

- **Restlessness:** The feeling of restlessness also comes with anxiety. Your mind usually gets agitated in stressful situations as a lot of changes are taking place at the same time. To deal with that, a feeling of restlessness also comes naturally. This feeling of restlessness is generally induced by the mind to keep you in a state of readiness.

- **The Feeling of Insecurity:** It is very common to have a feeling of insecurity in stressful situations. Stress makes you doubt most of the things as your mind is overactive in planning strategies to escape the situation.

- **Irritability:** Feeling irritated in a stressful situation is not very uncommon. It happens as your mind is busy focusing on essential issues. However, in the case of chronic stress, irritability becomes a part of nature. Their minds are so preoccupied with stress all the time that they can get irritated over anything. Their cognitive ability to process other things goes down considerably.

- **Heightened Sense of Positivity:** This may sound unusual, but it happens. Some with greater emotional stability react to stress in a very positive manner. Their mind is constantly trying to find a way around the problem, and they remain highly positive. They exhibit negligible signs of panic and command great control over situations. However, this is more common in short, stressful situations. Maintaining positivity in chronic stress is difficult. Yet, some people can train their minds to be calm and positive in every kind of situation. They remain non-judgmental of the situations and just treat them as regular incidents to keep their calm and composure. It is a positive habit that can be cultivated through mindfulness, and we will discuss it in detail further in the chapter. It can help you in keeping your calm and fighting stress better.

- **Depression:** Depression is a common side effect of chronic stress. When people face some sustained loss, they are unable to overcome it and start reliving it time and again. This can lead to depression. Letting the stressor affect you repeatedly is a poor choice, and it happens when people stop trying to overcome the problem. Depression has become very common these days, and people have started treating it as another common ailment, although it isn't. Depression can begin the process of total disintegration of mind, body, and spirit. Coming out of depression can be tough for many people, but there are several resources available that can help in overcoming depression, and all must be used in a systematic manner to come out of its trap.

- **Anger:** Frustration of being trapped in a stressful situation can lead to bouts of anger. The mind remains engaged in a vicious cycle and finds itself trapped. This can lead to anger. Proper stress management techniques can help in overcoming this problem.

- **Fatigue:** This is a very common thing that you may experience in case of chronic stress. The stress puts the body in a high alert mode, and that is an energy-consuming job. If this situation becomes steady as it does in case of chronic stress, one can start feeling the fatigue all the time. There may be a visible disinterest in doing anything.

- **Sadness:** Feeling melancholic is not very unusual in case of chronic stress. A sense of helplessness engulfs the victims, and they feel sad about their current state. The state of sadness is also due to their inability to get out of it.

- **Concentration Issues:** Facing concentration lapse issues is common as people generally find their minds too engrossed with the current problems. The mind remains so fixated on the stress that it stops paying attention to other things that need your attention. This leads to serious concentration problems. You may start remaining lost in thoughts most of the time, unable to fix your attention at one point.

2. Behavioral Impact

Our behavior is a reflection of our mental state. If we are in a state of chronic stress, the impact would be clearly visible in our behavior. This is something that might even be visible to others. Although these signs can be common for many problems but a combination of several signs is a clear indicator that a person is going through chronic stress and may need help.

- **Sudden Anger Outbursts:** It is very common for people to react to stress with anger. When people are not able to deal with stressful situations, they start demonstrating aggression. This is their own way of trying to take control of the situation; however, it seldom works. Sudden anger outbursts that may include punching things, throwing objects, and other such unruly behavior might even take the form of general aggression in the attitude. Although not uncommon, this is an incorrect way to deal with stress. It takes away your focus from the main problem, and you remain fixated on venting out your reaction. This attitude can also take the form of volatile mood swings where you can completely lose control of the way you might behave and can harm yourself or others. The best way out is to learn stress management techniques so that this energy and expression can be channelized in other constructive forms.

- **Addiction:** It is very common to look for stress-busting avenues when they are under surmounting pressure. Tobacco, cigarettes, alcohol, and drugs top the chart in this list; however, addiction to coffee also cannot be left out. All these things may provide momentary relief as they lower your stress response, but it is very easy to get addicted to them, and they can begin another set of problems too. While fighting with chronic stress, you will also have to fight with addiction, which might make the fight very tough. Addiction is one of the worst behavioral impact of stress on a person's life. It must be avoided at all costs as it further weakens your cognitive abilities to fight stress and increases your dependability on the addiction, which is eroding in itself. Therapy and various relaxation techniques can help you in getting out of the vicious cycle of addiction and chronic stress.

- **Insomnia:** Inability to sleep is yet another common problem associated with the stress of all kinds. The mind starts playing the stressful situation time and again, making you insecure and frightened. While in the humdrum of the day, these thoughts remain suppressed, they become prominent at night, making sleep very difficult. People either experience low quality sleeps with nightmares, or they are unable to sleep at all making their minds even more tired. Bouts of insomnia can be triggered by various incidents, and if not addressed properly, they can become difficult to handle. Meditation, visualization, and sleep hypnosis are some of the techniques that can help you in dealing with insomnia effectively. They also help in lowering the stress levels and induce relaxation.

- **Difficulty in Staying Awake for Long:** The human mind is strange, and while some people might find it difficult to sleep in stressful situations, others may find it difficult to stay awake when they are in deep stress, especially in the day. It also happens when you have a great workload, and you feel that you'll not be able to finish it anyway. The mind simply surrenders to the idea and starts inducing forceful sleep as an excuse. It may come in the form of lethargy and inability to stay awake during the day. Such issues can also be countered with the help of relaxation techniques and mindfulness.

- **Sudden Food Cravings or Sudden and Steep Changes in Eating patterns:** Same as sleeping, stress can have a completely opposite impact on appetite. While some people resort to emotional eating when in deep stress, others may find themselves unable to eat anything at all, sudden changes in eating patterns is an indicator that your body is experiencing extreme stress. You must take cognizance of the fact and simply not get swayed by the urges. Emotional eating can be very harmful, and it may numb your responses. Stress eating is an actual and dangerous phenomenon. The stress hormone cortisol motivates you to eat more and more high sugary foods that come under the category of comfort foods. These foods lead to the release of a comforting hormone that makes your brain feel a bit better. However, the relaxation is short-lived, and you'd need to pump more and more sugary food more often. Food cravings and hunger would increase considerably, and it would again begin a vicious cycle. If sudden changes in eating patterns are observed, it is important to handle them wisely through exercise, meditation, and social support.

- **Social Withdrawal:** It is very common for people facing chronic stress to become reclusive. This happens as their self-esteem and confidence take a severe hit. They start feeling the inability to cope with the social pressures and want to dodge questions that may be asked to them. Techniques like meditation, visualization, social support can help them in opening up.

- **Relationship Issues:** Chronic stress can cause relationship problems. As a result of stress, people stop trusting others and aren't able to confide. This also creates communication issues. All these things can be a big problem, and many people feel their relationships crumbling under the pressure of chronic stress. They start distrusting and develop contempt as they feel that others are not trying to understand them without ever really discuss their problems.

All these behavioral changes are a sign of chronic stress seeping into life. If you feel the symptoms creeping into your own life or in the life of someone else, you must become aware and take some actions. Many a time, finding the real stressor can be tough and you may never really experience anything drastic. However, that doesn't mean you can get trapped in the vicious stress cycle. It is always better to be watchful of the signs.

3. Physiological Impact

As we have already discussed, people generally treat stress to be an emotional or mental phenomenon. However, its physiological impact is even deeper. It has a deep physiological impact that can affect various vital functions. Chronic stress can degrade your health and make it difficult for you to recover. It leads to several chronic issues like hypertension, diabetes, obesity, and cardiovascular problems that simply don't go away or are very hard to go.

Some signs of stress are apparent, and they must never be ignored. If you start experiencing them very often or the signs persist, you must become aware and start taking preventive steps immediately.

- **Headaches:** Headaches are common in case of stress as the brain is on high alert. Chronic stress can intensify the headaches as the mind stops getting any respite from the stress at all.

- **Sweating:** You may witnesses sweating as soon as you are over with a stressful situation. The body releases a lot of built-up pressure, and sweating is a result of it.

- **Nervous Twitching:** It is also a sign of stress as there can be slight muscle spasm that may lead to twitching. Your body is furiously trying to make you aware of the stressful situation and indicating you to remain alert.

- **Pins and Needles:** This is also a sensation people often feel when they have got over a stressful situation. When you are in a stressful situation, the blood flow to various parts gets restricted as the muscles are getting all the blood. When you get over the stressful situation, the blood flow resumes to other parts, too, and you may experience the sensation as if pins and needles are being pierced. There is a slight tingling sensation.

- **Upset Stomach:** Stomach cramps and upset stomach also signal stress. People suffering from inflammatory bowel syndrome are more likely to suffer from stomach cramps and upset stomach under chronic stress as their colon is more sensitive.

- **Pain in the Back or Chest:** Anxiety can lead to pain in the chest and the back. The pain can be sharp and shooting or may even be mild and persistent. This can be alarming for people suffering from heart ailments as the pain may resemble a heart attack.

- **Cramps or Muscle Spasms:** The muscles get tense due to stress, and that can lead to cramps or muscle spasms.

- **Loss of Libido or Erectile Dysfunction:** Chronic stress can have a detrimental impact on a person's sex life. Women under chronic stress tend to lose their libido, and men also face erectile dysfunction. This problem needs to be understood clearly, and corrective measures are important. If the problem is ignored, it may spiral out of hand.

- **High Blood Pressure:** High blood pressure is a serious result of chronic stress. The blood circulation gets affected during stress, and if the stress is chronic, it can lead to high blood pressure. Medical intervention may be needed in time to handle the issue properly.

- **Heart Diseases:** Stress also has a deep impact on your heart. The blood vessels get contracted, and the heart has to work harder than necessary. If the problem persists for long, that may also lead to various heart problems.

- **Poor Immunity:** Stress beefs up the immune system, but if the stress becomes chronic, the immune system stops responding properly, and your defenses become weak. You become prone to various illnesses as your immune system is no longer working as it should.

The physiological impact of chronic stress is sustained, and it can cause great damage. It is important that you don't ignore the problems and address the problems causing chronic stress. There are ways through which stress can be reduced, and you can induce relaxation. To lower the stress, it is important that you understand the major causes of stress and identify your own stressors so that the resolution is effective.

Causes of Stress

In this part, we will look at some major things that cause stress in our daily lives. Work and personal life trigger the highest amount of stress. There are several things that may happen at your workplace and home that may cause stress. However, it is important that you identify the usual stressors so that you are better prepared to handle it.

The work-life has become very demanding these days. There is an insurmountable pressure that all of us face at work. Missing deadlines or not able to perform as per expectation can lead to great stress. The things mentioned below can lead to stress at work. If not addressed on time, they can take the form of chronic stress.

Common Causes of Stress at Work

- Excessive workload or too much responsibility
- Long and unproductive/unrewarding working hours
- Poor time/work management
- Lack of say in the decision-making process
- Job insecurity
- Discrimination at the workplace
- Harassment at the workplace
- Dangerous or unhealthy work conditions
- The feeling of being suppressed
- Overall discontentment from the current work

Common Causes of Stress in Personal Life

- Bereavement or loss of a loved one
- Increasing financial obligations
- No control over finances
- Divorce or marital discord
- Fear of financial insecurity
- Chronic illness or injury

- The obligation of someone sick in the family
- Moving to a new place
- The stress of marriage or any other long-term commitment
- Emotional issues
- Past traumatic events

These are the major causes of stress in life. However, stress is a perceived threat, and it is not important to have a real or physical reason to have stress. Even your mind can be a reason for all your stress, and that can be even more dangerous as that would have no limits. Some other things that can lead to chronic stress are:

Unrealistic Expectations: Being a perfectionist is a good thing, but expecting everything to go as per your expectations every time is unwise. Life, as we know, is uncertain and influenced by various external factors. If you start stressing out at every incident not going as planned, you are sure to get chronic stress.

Now before you start brushing this aside as a stupid thing to do, I would like to reflect a bit on your own life. Please recall all the instances when you had lost temper because someone else didn't do his/her job well or didn't turn up on time. It is one of the most common things to happen to us and causes a lot of stress in real life. We all have misconceptions about our own temperament. Such things that cause stress don't get noticed, but they are there.

- Think of getting served a bit late at a diner
- Having to wait longer than usual at a traffic signal because the driver in front of you wasn't moving
- Feeling irritated because the kids are extra playful at an event

These are simple examples of some of the common things that keep happening regularly, but we don't notice. There's no doubt that these things only cause acute stress. Now, simply consider facing such acute stress several times a day. The scenario wouldn't remain that pleasant.

Pessimistic and Worrying Attitude: Our attitude plays a very important role in ensuring our well-being. Through an optimistic attitude, we can even come out of the most troubling situations or at least give the best try. But, if the attitude is pessimistic, even a slight bump may start looking like the end of it. People with pessimistic and worrying attitudes don't think about finding a solution. They start exploring all the bad things that can happen from that point forward.

If they lose a job, they wouldn't even consider trying to find a new one but would be more worried that they may never get hired anymore. Their mind is simply thinking about all things that can go wrong. If you want to live a stress-free life, this is the attitude you need to avoid.

Unreasonable Threat Perception: Threat perception is a power we have developed through the complex process of evolution. It gives us an edge in survival. It enables us to deduce the things that can go wrong so that we are able to prepare and brace ourselves better. However, things start to go wrong when we start looking for a threat where there is none.

Airplanes can crash. That's a fact. But, does this mean that you'll hold it as an eventuality bound to happen anytime you fly. That's unreasonable threat perception. Unfortunately, many people are victims of this condition. They simply gather worries around them and then live in chronic stress. This tendency can severely restrict your ability to enjoy life, and you may spend your entire life in constant fear. To an extent, we all have this tendency, but it generally doesn't affect us that much. Many of us check the door locks twice or keep worrying whether we locked properly or not. We excessively worry about the safety of our kids. We worry about our finances. It's all fine to a reasonable extent. But, it is important to understand that things can be kept under complete only to a certain extent, and worrying excessively isn't going to do any good; on the contrary, it can be detrimental to our mental and physical health.

Till here, we have explored what, why, and how of stress. Stress is not an external phenomenon but our internal reaction to unfavorable or adverse conditions. It starts within us, and hence, it can be addressed.

Living in stress is not a compulsion. You can empower yourself and get out of it. It is very much possible to get out of stress.

The next part would help you in understanding the ways to get out of stress.

Chapter 2:Overcoming Stress

Identifying Stressors in Life

The first thing to do is to accept that stress is a part of life. People believe that if they can somehow remove stress from their life, they can be really happy and content. This idea has a core problem; you cannot remove stress completely from your life. Stress is not an external force; it is your reaction to an external change.

The best you can do is change the way you react to such situations.

So, the simple solution to this complex problem lies in recognizing the things that cause stress in life and change your attitude so that you are less affected by them.

The things that can stress us can be broadly divided into two categories:

1. **Internal Stressors:** Your mind has a big role to play in it. These stressors include your worries, existing psychological issues, past traumatic experiences that you are trying to avoid thinking about, behavioral patterns, and existing health-related issues.

2. **External Stressors:** Over these stressors, you can't really exercise any control, but learning to cope with them is easy, as avoiding them is always an option you can exercise to a great extent.

The important thing is to learn to deal with stressors. You must learn to identify the stressors and work with them in a correct manner.

For the sake of convenience, we can further divide the stressors into two categories:

1. **Changeable Stressors:** Most of the stress in our life is a result of our own careless attitude. We don't pay attention to things and get anxious when they get blown out of proportion. Simple things in our personal and professional lives can make a lot of difference if we learn to deal with them properly. We will term them as changeable stressors. We will learn ways to identify them and make course corrections.

2. **Unchangeable Stressors:** There are certain things that are beyond our control now. Past traumatic events that have happened, loss of loved ones, and other similar things which you can't change now, but they still stress you. We will learn the ways to deal with these stressors too. It may sound difficult, and in fact, it is, but by

acknowledging and accepting those things, it is possible to move on even from those stressors. Meditation, guided imagery, yoga, and other relaxation techniques can help you a lot in moving on.

Identifying and Working on Changeable Stressors

We all have scores of common stressors in daily life that we are unaware of. It is important to identify things that stress you and correct them.

Some of the common stressors are:

Urgency and Haste: We are living in a really fast-paced world. If our forefathers could come and witness the kind of life we are living, I'm sure they'd find it giddying. We are always in such a haste. There are always deadlines that can't be met. We are always running as we are getting late. We are always running out of time. We never care to stop for a moment and think that it isn't something forced by others. We are the ones responsible for our plight. We are trying to bite more than we can chew, and that's the reason for all the chaos. The result is an urgency that's causing more harm than anything else. When we show haste, our stress hormones go up, and it stirs us physiologically and emotionally. Doing haste is a life and death situation is one thing and always being in haste is another. It gives way to recklessness, which is again very bad. If you want to bring down stress in your life, you will have to work on the urgency and haste factor in your life. Take the amount of work you can finish and work on it with focus while there is still time left. This would bring down stress to a great extent.

Poor Time Management: Deadlines are a part of the work culture now. There is no point in getting affected by deadlines. The important thing is to work as per the deadlines. Stop pushing work to the end of the deadline. People think that they can somehow finish the work even at the end of the deadline and they very well may be able to do it. But, they forget that when the clock is ticking like a timebomb, the stress level in their body is also high. Simply changing your attitude towards deadlines and proper time management can eliminate a lot of stress from your life.

Taking More Work than You can Handle: The desire to become an overachiever is very common. People simply take more work than they can handle and then start feeling crushed under its weight. Neither they are able to impress, nor they are able to remain happy. It is important to understand your physical and mental limits and respect them if you want to reduce stress in your life.

Clutter: Keeping clutter around can be a major cause of stress. If your house or work table is cluttered, you are most likely to feel out of control. Clutter hinders your ability to see the big picture clearly. You are also unable to prioritize things as several things are lying around in an unorganized manner. If you want to regain control of your life, it is very important to declutter. Either it is your house, workplace, or your mind, decluttering can be the key to de-stressing.

Vicious Anger Trap: Stress in life can be very frustrating, both emotionally and physiologically. When you are facing chronic stress, you are most likely to feel frustrated and angry. However, people seldom realize that this very anger can be a reason they are unable to get out of stress. It is a behavioral change that takes your grip away from emotional control, and you get caught in the trap of chronic stress. It's like you feel angry because you are stressed, and you will remain stressed because you are angry and hence, unable to think clearly and logically.

All these are changeable stressors. We don't realize, but we have the ability to change them whenever we want. The solution may look oversimplified, but it is the most effective way to start de-stressing your life.

To change something big, you essentially don't need to make drastic changes. Making some simple foundational changes in the basic structure can also do the job. These 5 simple things can take away a lot of stress from your life, and they are very much in your hand.

As we discuss, stress management in personal and professional life, you will see that these stressors would come up again and again as they are part of the basic structure and hold great importance in reducing stress in life.

Managing Stress at Work Place

I have intentionally taken stress at work before stress at home. We spend the highest amount of our wake time either at the workplace or thinking about work. Most of the stressors are in some way connected to work, and hence, it is important that stress management at work is given priority.

Organize and De-clutter: Clutter is one of the biggest reasons for stress at work. It is something which is in front of you, but you never really place it as the cause of stress. When your work desk is cluttered, it becomes really difficult to organize things. If you want to reduce stress in your life, the first thing you must do is clean your desk. Simply remove everything except what's required to work. Don't keep files and folders on the work desk. Pens, paper clips, coffee mugs, clock, scheduler, everything needs to go.

- If you work on a computer, everything besides your computer must go.
- Find a specific place for everything.

- A separate cabinet for files which you need regularly and another for the ones you don't need very often.
- Do the same on your computer. Make clearly labeled folders, and don't let you're your desktop be a fish market. There are people who might need a few minutes to locate a specific file or folder on their desktop screen as the whole world is just lying there. Don't be that person.
- Clean your table and your desktop first thing in the morning and at the end of the day. Make it a ritual.

This is a very simple and easy solution and may not look very effective at the moment. However, you'll realize its importance once you put it to use. It will not only save a lot of your time but would also bring down your stress level. When things are scattered around us, they cause latent stress. The stress is not visible, but it is always present, and it is more harmful.

The simple process of decluttering your workplace can help you in reducing stress.

Schedule Things: Make a list of the tasks to be completed in a day. It is very simple, and until you are not on a war front, the day in an office is quite predictable. This means you can easily make a list of the things to be finished in a day. Now, as you keep finishing a task, your work stress would start going down. You'd clearly know the number of things you have already finished and the number of tasks pending. This would also instill confidence inside you and also make you more accountable.

Prioritize: Some people have a misconception that they can work like warriors. They would face things as they come. Such people are never able to enjoy their lives fully as something urgent would always come up when they want to take a break. Our mind has a lot more work to do than you can think. It is easy for it to prioritize something else and put important office work on the backburner. This can cause a lot of stress. You would be doing the same amount of work and yet would never be at peace.

Subdivide the work into categories like urgent, important, and less important. Start working as per the urgency, and hence, you can avoid finishing things in haste. Doing everything on the deadline is a habit that most people pick up in the course of their careers, and it is responsible for causing the highest amount of stress. It forces you to work late and work more while the quality of work gets compromised as your main focus is on finishing the job.

Avoid Distractions: Most of us like to think that we get more work than we can do. We genuinely feel so without counting the actual number of productive hours put into work.

Japanese people are known for their work culture. The employees give in extra hours to work. In fact, going home on time is considered bad or even unprofessional. People usually work from 10-14 hours every day. They also don't take week-offs and never more than one. But, does that mean a person putting in extra hours of work is actually doing more work. Recently, Microsoft did an experiment at its Japanese plant. It forced its employees to stick to 8 hours of work every day and even gave long-weekends of 3 days every week. Surprisingly the production at its plant went up by 40%. The reason was simple: the employees felt less stressed at work and more inspired. They had no obligation to stay late. They stopped wasting time and committed themselves to work.

Most people unknowingly waste a lot of time in distractions. Checking Facebook notifications and uploading Instagram selfies takes up a lot of time. You may feel that it only takes up a few seconds, but that's never the truth. Every break creates a distraction, and getting back to work takes much longer. Soon you start feeling tired and lose interest in work.

If you work without distractions, you would be able to finish the work much faster and wouldn't feel the stress of work.

Live in the Present: This is another problem that causes the highest amount of stress. People are more worried about the future than they care for their present. This even takes away the effort from the present. Live in the present and focus on the work at hand. Stop worrying about the outcome as it is never solely in your hand, and external factors are at work. However, if you keep worrying, your present effort would also get affected and would increase your stress.

Tackle the Bigger Obstacles First: It is always the best to get the harder things out of your way, and then you can work without much stress. This also gives you the advantage of time. If the harder task is going to take time longer than anticipated, you wouldn't be squandering on a deadline. This helps in lowering stress at the workplace.

Take Periodic De-Stressing Breaks: It has been scientifically proven that sitting for long periods can cause physical and mental stress. Make it a habit to take stretching breaks after a certain period of time. This not only keeps your mind and body relaxed but also helps in focusing better on the work.

Set Realistic Goals: We often feel discontent when we set unrealistic goals. It is everyone's right to desire the best, but expecting the same to take place is a recipe for disaster. You can't start competing with everyone else at your workplace and be envious of them. This will simply shoot your stress through the roof. It is very important that you set realistic goals. Objectively look at your work and only expect things to happen on average. If you don't set your expectations very high, you'd feel less stressed at things happening or not happening around you.

Workdays can be very long. Sometimes it starts feeling as if you have been working for eternity. Such a feeling can cause stress. This especially happens when you are on projects that you don't like much but don't have an option to avoid.

On a day to day basis, there can be several things that you can do to keep the stress levels at work low.

Don't Overeat: Overeating during the day is something that happens quite often but never catches anyone's attention. Overeating can be a cause of physical and mental stress at work. It can work negatively on so many levels. When you overeat, you can start feeling lethargic and may find it difficult to finish your tasks. It can make you unenthusiastic, and there is a reason for it. When you are hungry, your gut releases a hunger hormone called ghrelin. This hormone helps in maintaining high activity levels and also keeps your mind alert. When you overeat, the ghrelin levels go down for long, and the satiety hormone called leptin takes its place. It leads to a feeling of comfort and can make work difficult. To keep the day going smoothly in a stress-free manner, it is important that you eat light.

Take Coffee Breaks in Groups: This can sound counterproductive on many levels. However, studies have proven this fact indisputably that taking coffee breaks in groups can help you in releasing stress and pent-up tension at work. Consuming too much coffee can be harmful, but taking coffee breaks with your colleagues can help you in improving your mood.

Slow Down a Bit: Most people don't realize the importance of relaxation breaks. They feel it will break their flow or waste their time. Relaxation breaks don't need to be very long. You can simply close your eyes for a minute and let your body lose. This brief break can help you in releasing a lot of pressure. You'd feel more energized and clear. You must remember that while you take a physical break, your mind is still working, and it gets time to strategize in a better way. Taking these breaks frequently would help you in keeping your stress levels low.

No Shame in Apologizing Genuinely: You may find it hard to gulp, but please lend me your ears. One of the biggest reasons for stress in the workplace is the pride war. Things may happen in which sometimes you may be at fault, and you may find it difficult to admit. This can lead to stress building inside you as there is always a fear that things can go out of hand. The others may also start finding excuses to bring it up, and that would also lead to stress buildup. The best option always is to genuinely apologize for your mistake at the first instant and get over with it. You can end the whole episode then and there with a simple admission. It can work wonders on your stress.

Vacations are Important: Some people are so caught up with their work and stressed that they don't realize the importance of taking complete breaks. A complete disassociation from work can make you more sincere and increase your productivity. It would also give you a chance to wind down and would lower your stress levels.

Managing Stress in Personal Life

Our personal lives are no less complicated and can be powerful stress generators. There are simple habits that we pick over time, which can lead to a lot of stress. For instance, spending time on social media platforms. When it started, people thought they had got an amazing way to connect to our near and dear ones. Lo and behold, it has made us distant from everyone now. It is a platform that only leads to the generation of contempt and discontent.

Not only this, we spend a large amount of our time on these platforms that should have gone into constructive things.

This is just one habit that's generating a lot of stress in our lives. There are several other habits that are picked up for relaxing but do just the opposite.

Some of them are:

Emotional Eating: We have already covered the aspect of emotional eating as an effect of high stress. Food is relaxing and can provide momentary comfort, but it isn't the solution. In fact, it can begin several problems that you wouldn't want to handle.

Picking up food as a means to relax is a bad idea. Don't go that way. Don't go for comfort foods as they would induce food cravings, and they are unhealthy. The dopamine release caused by sweets and chocolates is temporary and harmful. If food is the first thing you look for after coming from your office irrespective of hunger levels, then you need to get alert.

Smoking and Alcohol: Addiction is a bad thing, and it never provides a solution. It would only lead to more and more stress. Period.

Procrastination: After a hectic day at work, who doesn't want to relax. We all feel that we can push the work at home aside as we are not answerable to a boss at home. This is a poor attitude and would lead to stress. Procrastination can easily become a habit and would keep causing stress in one way or another. Home is as important as work, and if there is some work, it needs to be completed.

Sitting in front of the TV for Long Hours: This is again a habit that many people pick up. They simply come home and sit glued in front of the idiot box without considering the quality of the content or their own interest. Long TV viewing hours can also cause physical and mental stress. There is a lot of content for which your mind is either not ready or doesn't want it, but sitting helplessly in front of the TV, you can't help but absorb it.

Mobile or Internet Addiction: This is again a problem that has sprung up recently. People just love to fiddle with their phones. They feel that it provides a good distraction from stress. They are wrong. They are simply refusing to acknowledge the stress denying it the required vent. This is even more dangerous. The same problems that are associated with TV viewing also plague the Smartphone and internet users, and hence, they face a double whammy.

It is VERY IMPORTANT to give your stress the right vent. People feel that as they are tired, they simply need to lie down, and this would relax them. They are wrong. The stress usually isn't physical, and hence, lying down doesn't help much. In fact, light physical activity after coming home can be wonderful. Go for a walk, cook your favorite disk, play some physical sport, or talk to someone but give you're your body a real chance to wind down.

Quality Sleep is Essential

It is important that you prepare your body to have a good night's sleep. If there is physical or mental stress, either the quality of sleep would be poor, or you won't be able to sleep at all, and both the things will have an adverse impact on your overall stress levels.

It is not only the time of sleep but the quality of restful sleep you have that matters for lowering the stress levels. Besides other factors, your physical relaxation has an important role to play in it.

There are several minute changes that you can bring in your day to day life that can help in bringing down stress in personal life.

Some of them are:

Undertake De-stressing Physical Activity: As we have already discussed, we may feel tired. The exhaustion is generally mental and not physical. If you engage in any kind of physical activity, it can give your stress the right vent and help you in de-stressing. Choose your personal way of winding down. Go for a long walk, play some sport, go swimming, or cook something. You can even do all of these things periodically. These activities help in melting the stress. They take your mind completely away from the things that might be a cause of frustration and tension. Even a short respite from the stress can help you in gaining a better perspective of the problem.

Seek Ultimate Relaxation: There are several things that are so overpowering that they don't let your attention sway. Playing with a young kid, a pet, or sitting and talking with a loved one can be one among them. Find the thing that has the power to divert your attention and relax you completely. It can be anything. If simply walking in the sand can relax you completely, so be it.

Work on Love: There is no denying the fact that there cannot be a better antidote of stress than love. Both have the power to cut each other. High stress in life can drain the love out of you, but the vice-versa is also completely true. The choice is yours. If you want to lower the stress in your life, keep working on your love. Besides everything else, pay attention to your love and relationship. The stronger the love bond you have with someone, the easier it would be for you to de-stress.

Sex is a Great Stress Buster: Sex is again a form of intense physical and emotional activity that can bring down stress in your life. It helps you in relaxing completely. Regular and passionate sex can help in lowering the stress levels in your body.

Music: Listening to music or playing some instrument can also help you in giving a vent to your stress and relaxing. Music is not only relaxing to the ears, but it is also very soothing to the soul.

Make Positive Changes to Your Diet: Oily and greasy food brought from the fast-food chains may look appetizing, but it cannot provide the nutrition required to help you get over stress. Remember that stress is not only emotional but physical. A poor diet can also lead to great stress. Start including healthy food options in your diet. If you want to lower stress, try to eat as fresh food as you can lay your hands on. Fruits and vegetables are the best, to begin with. Try to go for organic foods. Do not load empty calories into your system and adopt a healthy diet.

Your diet must also include things that provide Vitamin C, Vitamin B2, and Vitamin B6. Along with that, eat foods that have a lot of calcium and magnesium.

Lower Coffee Intake: This is an open fact that overdependence on coffee can also lead to stress. There are plenty of healthy options like fruit smoothies and green tea. They can help you in feeling fresh and would also be beneficial.

Exercise: Doing some kind of exercise regularly in the morning and evening can help you in keeping the stress levels to a minimum. Aerobic exercises, yoga, or even a simple walk can do the trick. They all can help you in keeping your mind in the right place.

Meditate: There is nothing like meditation when it comes to reducing stress. It is a simple technique that helps in keeping the mind calm and lowers the stress to a great extent. We will be discussing meditation in detail further in the book.

Managing the Mind

In the beginning, I compared stress to inflammation. Both have several uncanny similarities. However, there's one major difference; there is a limit to the damage inflammation can cause as it is a physical phenomenon. Stress is largely in our minds, which is limitless, and hence, the amount of damage stress can cause is unbound.

The mind is the most important avenue to take care of when it comes to stress. The stress is simply a perceived threat, and there is no limit to the amount of fear your mind can create. If the mind is hell-bent on frightening you, it can make you feel threatened by a cockroach, which is literally helpless in front of you. Did that hit home?

It's a fact that there is literally no reason for people to fear roaches as they pose no imminent danger. The infection and all is understandable, but still, there is nothing a cockroach can do to cause immediate harm. Yet, people start jumping at the sight of a cockroach.

A stressed mind can start doing that for everything. Suppose you come back from an interview, and your mind simply starts playing everything that went bad on a loop. Not getting a job wouldn't even be anywhere close to that experience. This is the power of the mind in creating perceived threats, even in simple things. When there are unchangeable factors involved like traumatic events of the past, the mind can get very nasty. From frequent flashbacks, visualizations, to nightmares, the extent to which the mind can get to make you frightened is unimaginable.

The mind uses this fear as a tool to keep you away from falling into any such danger away. It wants to be in a comfort zone. It is simply a survival mechanism. However, it cannot be a way to live a fruitful like. It is very important that you break out of this tendency and reclaim your life back.

If you don't exercise conscious control, it can blow even small incidents out of proportion and make them look enormous. Forgetting to switch off an electrical appliance is nothing so big that you need to remain fixated on it for the whole day. However, there are people who wouldn't be able to stop worrying about it. The same happens with people who very often feel that they haven't locked the door properly. You can keep worrying about the reaction of your boss on something the next day fully well knowing that you cannot exercise any control over it.

Before even venturing into this territory, it is important to realize that stress is nothing but your body's response to any perceived threat, and the 'perceived' is the guiding word here. It is something you are simply imagining. It is a made-up scenario. There is no real reason to fear it. Understanding the threat insideyour mind is the most important.

Positive Outlook can Help a Lot

There can be nothing better to fight stress than a positive outlook. A positive mindset can prove to be very helpful in reducing stress. Our mind has the ability to think both ways. It can lead the thoughts in a constructive, positive way or may drag them towards pessimism; the choice is yours. You will have to train your mind to think of the positive things that can come out of everything that stresses you out. This isn't a very difficult task. Even the most destructive things have positivity attached to them. The need is to look at them positively. You will have to change your perception of threat.

Stop Living in Constant Denial, Acknowledge and Accept

One of the biggest reasons of stress growing in our lives is our denial to acknowledge them. Anyone can have things in the past that are so bad that every time it comes to mind, it brings painful memories. But, does that mean that by not acknowledging that incident you can undo it. It is past, and this means that the incident has already taken place. It is time for you to acknowledge it and accept the incident. Learn from it if possible, to avoid it in the future. Living in denial is only going to make you more stressed. Ghosts only scare those people who believe in them are scared of them.

If there is some fear in your heart regarding some current event keeping it in your heart and not registering it properly is also not going to help. For example, is someone loved is battling a terminal illness, and you are afraid of the loss, you will have to acknowledge the possibility and accept fate. You can't live in denial. The sooner you come to terms with the reality that it can and will happen someday, the easier life would get for you. Your stress level would go significantly down.

The same happens for personal insecurities. If you are insecure about your job, either you can keep feeling stressed about it without accepting it on merit, or you can start planning for a better one or start improving yourself. If you give a thought to it, the options are plenty. But, the options would never look viable until you start giving them a thought, and even for that, acknowledging and accepting the problem is important.

Avoid the Stressors

Once you have identified the stressors in your life, you can try to avoid the things and scenarios that can lead to stress to a great extent. Believe me, sometimes, it is not going to be easy. But it is the right thing to do.

There are certain stressors that you can clearly and easily avoid. Traffic, loud places, commotion, clutter, deadline rush as these are in your hands to a great extent. You would need to prepare in advance. You may even have to work a bit extra, but you can be sure that there would be much less stress in life.

However, there are times when the stressors are beyond your control. If someone else is causing friction, humiliation, or aggression, it is normal for a person to feel stressed. When not in a position of power, people choose to bear the insult, and this leads to stress buildup. Most people find it an easy way out, as raising their concerns can be counterproductive.

It is a decision you will have to make for yourself. You can choose to let the stress build inside you and risk an outburst sometime else or someone else. You can also choose to voice your concern on the right platform or leave the place, which is causing so much stress. The latter options will give your stress a positive outlet while the former will only lead to negative outbursts.

When you are able to voice your concerns in the right manner, you feel more positive and confident. It helps you to release even more stress.

Therefore, try to bypass the stressors so that you don't feel agitated in the normal course of life. When avoiding them isn't possible, face the stressors in a positive way.

Adapt

There would be some stressors that you acknowledge but have no way to avoid. Like living in a noisy neighborhood. There is a limit to the number of complaints you can register. In such a scenario, can you let the stress take over? No, this is not a viable option. If you are stressed by the noise, use noise-canceling headphones, or adequate soundproofing, you can also create your own diversion. Paying attention to the stressor and fretting about it is only going to increase the stress inside you.

Life is simply an art of continuous learning, and coping with stress is an ongoing process. You simply can't allow petty things to take over your peace of mind and life. It is important that you regain control, and the moment you do that, there would be no reason for stress. Remember, stress is simply a response of your body to an uncontrolled situation or event.

5 Major Mental Stressors

Besides external factors, the mind is responsible for creating most of the stressors. If you want to manage your mind, it is important to 5 basic stressors created by the mind. These are basically mindsets that influence the way you lead your life. They have a strong influence on your behavior, and if you don't pay attention, they will cause stress in several ways.

If you are able to find your way around these stressors, you will also be able to lower stress in your life significantly.

1. **My way or Highway Attitude:** It's difficult to digest, but people do have this authoritarian attitude in general. Again you may feel that the percentage of people having this attitude may be minuscule. You are up for a surprise. Most of us have and exhibit this attitude. The only difference is that we only show it to people over whom we exercise considerable control, for example, kids, spouses, family members, subordinates, etc.

The biggest problem with this attitude is of having a high level of expectations that are bound to remain unfulfilled, and then the resulting stress would hit you like a hammer. It would be followed by rage, remorse, contempt, and several other such feelings. Whatever the consequences, the damage would be done as your stress level would flare up anyway. This condition can easily become chronic as people start expecting the same even from others, and then they face even greater disappointments.

People start the world to run according to them. Even perfectionism is also an extension of this mindset, and it also causes the same amount of stress. It is important to accept the fact that individuals perform actions as per their convenience and will, and they can't be run in an authoritarian way. You can't run the whole world around like a military drill school and hence would have to stop behaving like a drill sergeant.

2. **Discontent and Contempt:** Another reason for stress in life is discontent. We are not satisfied with what we have. We want much more of it. We don't want to rest until we have all of it. If anyone else will have something more or better, we will have contempt, and both discontent and contempt would eventually cause stress in life. They push you towards the dark corners of self-pity.

The desire to continuously improve is a positive feeling, but to beat others for that is a regressive idea and would only increase the stress in life.

It is a mindset you must try to stay away from. The more discontent you have, the more stressful you'll feel.

3. **Self-Doubt:** Underconfidence is not uncommon. Most people fail at some point of time in their lives. In fact, the most glorious tales of success have also been even more glorious tales of failures. The only difference between them and others is that they never gave up. When people laughed and mocked their failures, they learned from their mistakes, got up, and tried again. Their failures didn't shake their confidence. They didn't begin doubting their will and determination. You may lack the skill as it is something that you can learn and improve. But, you must always keep your determination steady. When people start having self-doubt, they come under stress. They start feeling stressed about everything.

   They not only feel stressed about their performance in every sphere of life but also feel stressed about the opinion of others about their performance. It is an imaginary territory with a scope of unimaginable fear and stress.

It is important that you always stay away from self-doubt. Work on your skills and keep your determination to succeed intact. If you start harboring self-doubt, stress will become an integral part of your life.

4. **Pessimism:** If you develop an attitude where you just want to look at things in a negative shade, there is no getting away from stress. The people who are looking at everything around them in a negative shade would worry nonetheless. Stress would become a common and integral part of their lives.

   Over-optimism is also not a very good thing, but you simply can't keep judging everything as it is going to go bust the next moment.

5. **Procrastination:** This is a mindset that can cause the highest amount of stress in personal and professional lives. Procrastination is one of the biggest causes of chronic stress. It is a mindset that makes you defy all the rules of happiness. You simply don't respect time, commitments, and work. Procrastinators are always busy making excuses. The time they consume in making an excuse could have been used for completing the work, but they would rather put it for later than do it.

   This mindset leads to a lot of stress, and it makes you sit on deadlines and puts you in bad books of a lot of people.

This is a mindset you must get over with as soon as possible if you want to reduce stress in life.

Ways to Deal with Unchangeable Stressors

Until this point, we have discussed at length about the changeable stressors. We understand that by changing our habits, mindset, ways, and choices, we can avoid them. We can also find ways around them. However, there are stressors that can't be changed and avoided. Such stressors can be traumatic incidents that have taken place in the past as well as permanent losses that can't be replaced like the loss of loved ones. Some unchangeable stressors are simply painful; with themselves, they bring feelings of pain and grief. But, there are a few unchangeable stressors that are horrific in nature. This means that they invoke memories that are difficult to bear. Memories of the past you don't want to relive ever but are flashed in front of your eyes randomly.

These stressors are inside us, and hence, they can't be avoided. There is no running away from them.

There are people who feel afraid to sleep as they fear to have those memories in front of them. Some people are afraid to stay in the dark. They are afraid of some past experiences. Victims of sexual abuse in their childhood get so much scarred that they find it difficult to get intimate with anyone else ever. Others can't come to terms that physical intimacy can even be pleasurable.

These are just some examples of unchangeable stressors, and the list is endless.

This is a fact that because the unchangeable stressors have already happened in the past, there is nothing you can do to undo them. Neither murdering the aggressor nor having more than you had lost could help in such a situation. This doesn't mean that living under such heavy stress is a viable option. This kind of chronic stress would have a deep impact on the victim's physical and mental health.

Yet, there are ways to deal with unchangeable stressors. Indeed, it is going to be difficult as the pain is very near to you. It isn't something you can do much about. The fear is also constant, and it is contagious in many ways. However, you can learn to live with such stressors and manage a considerably stress-free life.

1. Acknowledge and Accept the Stressors
2. Forgive and Let-Go
3. Engage in Activities That Would Express, Modify, or Distract the Feelings

One of the biggest problems in dealing with unchangeable stressors is that victims are afraid to acknowledge and accept the traumatic incidents that have taken place in the past. They want to avoid having to relive those experiences time and again, and this makes up for most of the trouble.

If a pigeon closes its eyes on facing a cat, does this make the pigeon invisible?

Definitely, the answer is no. The pigeon becomes an easy meal of the cat. The cat would have no guilty conscious or remorse about it.

If there are past traumatic experiences in your life, they will keep haunting you. There is simply no getting around the fact. Either you want to acknowledge and accept them or not.

However, if you take the help of counselors, therapists, and share your experiences, it can help you in accepting that the incident has happened and you have come far ahead of it. The same experiences may lose their intensity, and you'd have discussed their intensity several times over.

There is no denying the fact that the experience can be tough. However, it is one of the most reliable ways to free yourself from such incidents and dim the scars of the past.

Similarly, the people who are stressed due to the loss of their loved ones also can help themselves by talking about it extensively. Opening up about your feelings can help you in adopting a positive outlook. You may find it easier to do something constructive about your feelings and experiences.

Therefore, acknowledging and accepting the fact is the correct way to begin dealing with unchangeable stressors.

Forgive and Let-Go

Many people remain trapped in their past as they are simply unable to forgive their aggressors or don't let-go off the grudge ever. I know it is very easy to ask anyone to forgive an aggressor that may have permanently scarred your life. There are some grudges that you just can't let go. They become your obsession. You live with a simple one-point program to avenge one thing in your life. This very obsession with pain is the main problem. It is not the incident that's the cause of the problem now. It is your obsession with it that creates the problem. It becomes a part of identity, and you resist letting it go.

The best way to get over the problem is to forgive. You need to have mercy on yourself and forgive yourself for bearing it for so long. The aggressor doesn't have to do anything with it. In fact, the aggressor would never ever get affected even if you remain a victim for eternity. This simple realization is the most important.

So, the second step should be to forgive or let go of the incident. Accept that you have been living it unnecessarily for an unusually long time, and it is now time to move on.

Engage in Activities That Would Express, Modify, and Distract the Feelings

This is the final step of recovery and in fact, the easiest of the three. It is the most relieving step as most of the things are in your control. Once you have accepted the past and allowed it to fade away, you only need to work towards a faster recovery.

There are several techniques through which you can work on recovery:

Yoga: Yoga is a great way of physical and mental exercise. The breathing exercises in yoga and very helpful in overcoming stress and controlling the mind.

Meditation: Meditation is one of the most effective ways to stabilize the mind and bring your awareness to the right focus. If stress has been causing distress in your life, meditation can provide you great relief.

Visualization: Visualization is a technique that can be used to induce relaxation. With the help of various imageries, you can train your mind to accept and acknowledge the past and also learn to let it go.

Hypnosis: Hypnosis is a technique that involves guided thinking in order to make the victim relax completely. It helps in better sleeping and relaxation

These are the ways through which you will be able to express your feelings more clearly, modify your thought process or the way you have been dealing with certain things, and create positive distractions.

Simple Tips to Minimize Everyday Stress

There are some tips to minimize everyday stress. There is nothing out of the world in these techniques, and you may not even need any kind of help to perform them, but I can assure you that if you follow them, you will certainly feel a positive change in your stress levels.

- **Meditate:** This is one of the most powerful things you can bring into your life. Meditation will immensely help you in dealing with stress. It is a highly effective way to bring down stress in life. Some people that meditation can't do any kind of magic then why to sit in contorted positions for long periods. They are correct. Meditation would do no magic. But, meditation would surely help in changing your perception. It is a way to balance your mind. It gives you a genuine chance to look deep inside your mind and find the main causes of the problem. Once you have that kind of insight, solving the problem gets very easy. Therefore, if you really want to deal with stress, meditation should be on your priority list. In the next part of this book, we will be discussing meditation and all other stress-reducing techniques in detail.

- **Maintain a Journal of Positivity:** You can't remove darkness through the darkness, but even a small candle can help in removing darkness. A positive journal can have the impact of that candle. Life is full of experiences, and if you observe closely, there would be several experiences that can be called positive. Experiences that might have come unexpectedly. Incidents where people may have gone out of the way to help you. Instances when you might have felt very powerful and strong. Simply make it a habit to write down such instances. No matter what we do, there are times when we start feeling low again, in such dark and hopeless circumstances, that journal would work as the candle in the dark and give hope.

- **Exercise Daily:** Physical exercise is a great way to counter mental stress. These days our minds get tired very fast, but our body never really gets the exercise it needs, and this imbalance can cause sleep issues, irritation, and frustration. Daily exercise can help you in overcoming this problem. In spite of the physical work, you will feel more energetic and balanced. It would also take the stress away from your mind. It creates a positive distraction, and your mind has something else to think about besides the things that have been stressing it out.

- **Try Power Napping:** Power nap is a powerful tool to relieve stress. A 10-minute power nap can leave you refreshed, and you can observe your stress levels going down. The short duration of these naps makes them convenient, and they can be taken anywhere. If you ever start feeling very stressed during the day, try taking a power nap of 10 minutes.

- **Laugh Out Loud:** Laughter is the best medicine for any kind of stress. It also helps in bringing down stress, anger, and frustration. If you can laugh genuinely, then there can't be anything better than that, but expecting that in stressful situations wouldn't be good. Simply trying to laugh out loud in any kind of situation can bring your stress levels down. This is a technique you can try anywhere. In fact, laughing is a complete exercise in

Yoga, and its specific job is to bring down the stress level in individuals.

- **Develop a Hobby:** Developing a new hobby is constructive engagement, and it would definitely help you in lowering the stress levels. When you are trying to do something engaging or learn something that you like, your brain gets focused on it, and hence, the stress areas stop getting importance. The idler you are, the more stressful you'll feel. Therefore, it is very helpful if you can keep yourself constructively engaged.

- **Bring Home a Pet or Watch Pet Videos when Stressed:** Pets are great stressbusters. They have an infectious smile, and their love is also contagious. You can feel genuine love from the pets, which is free of any kind of deceit. Therefore, this love has the power to strike us deep. If you live alone or feel highly stressed, having a pet is a great idea. If due to any pressing reason, you can't have pets or have allergies, you can also watch pet videos on YouTube, and that also helps in bringing down the stress level.

- **Change Your Perspective:** Most of all, it is very important to change your perspective. If you keep looking at things in a negative way, the solution would never be in sight. Adopt a broader view of things and try to look at things in a positive light. Don't just look at things only in the negative light, have a 360-degree view of things, and it would help you tremendously.

- **Maintain Close Proximity to Nature:** There is no pacifier like nature. The vastness of nature has the power to bring down any kind of stress. It is so powerful that it can make anything look small. If you feel overwhelmed by your problems, simply try going in the lap of nature. Anyplace serene can help you in calming the mind completely, and you'll be able to think with greater clarity.

Chapter3: Relaxation and Stress Reduction Techniques

Deep Breathing

Deep breathing is a powerful way to calm the mind. Most people don't realize the power of breathing. Breath is the life source. You can't survive even for minutes without the breath. Your breath is your fastest interaction with this world, and it is the only thing that coming in and going out rapidly. If you can make the breath a medium to release stress, the exchange would become very easy.

Breathing has been in use as a calming technique for centuries. All ancient practices used deep breathing to stabilize the mind. Either it is yoga or meditation, breathing is an integral part of the practice.

Deep breathing is easy and very relaxing. It needs no special preparation, and it can be carried out anywhere anytime. The relief is instantaneous, and it would calm you down.

Whenever you feel stressed, you can practice deep breathing for comfort and stress reduction.

If you can find a secluded place, please go and sit there.

It is better to sit in a relaxed manner. If you are wearing tight-fitting clothes, simply loosen them a bit.

There is no specific position you need to take to practice deep breathing. You can sit on a chair. If you want, you can also lie down straight. When you lie down, place your arms beside your torso with palms facing up.

There are several ways in which deep breathing is practiced. Simply feeling the breath and letting it regain its natural pace helps you in relaxing.

If you are feeling very anxious and feel that you might have a panic attack, you can also practice controlled breathing.

The following example demonstrates both.

You can also record the following script in your own voice and play it for a guided breathing exercise.

Deep Breathing Practice

You can close your eyes gently for faster relief, or if you are feeling anxious you can also keep them open

Now, loosen yourself a bit

Let every part of your body relax

If you feel the tension in any specific part of your body simply try to move it slightly in its place to release the tension

There may be several thoughts in your mind

You don't need to worry about them

All the stress and anxiety is a part of life; it is important to accept it

Now is not the time to worry about it

It is time to focus on the most important aspect of life - Breathing

Bring all your awareness to the process of your breathing

Just focus on the way of your breathing

Are you breathing fast?

Is it slow?

Are you able to breathe rhythmically?

Don't judge the way you are breathing

Simply observe it

Breathing is a majestic process

We never pay attention to it

Pay attention to the way you are inhaling

The way each breath goes in

Travels through your whole respiratory system and then comes out

Nothing is hidden

The process is clear

Yet we never pay attention to it

Breathe in

Breathe out

Breathe in

Breathe out

Breathe in

Breathe out

Breathe in

Breathe out

Breathe in

Breathe out

There is no need to control anything

Let everything flow naturally

Let the life energy come in through your nostrils

Let this fresh air calm all the anxiety inside you

Breathe in

Breathe out

Breathe in

Breathe out

Breathe in

Breathe out

Again observe your breathing

Is it still rapid?

Has it regained its natural pace?

If you are still breathing rapidly

Simply keep breathing with focus

Breathe in

Breathe out

Breathe in

Breathe out

Breathe in

Breathe out

The breathing would calm your senses

It acts as a tranquilizer

It makes you feel more peaceful

Now we will practice deep breathing

You simply need to inhale very slowly

Inhale as much air as you can but be slow

There is no need to show any kind of haste

Just keep inhaling through your nose till you can't hold any more air

Then,

Even more slowly exhale through your mouth

While exhaling try to exhale as much air as you have inside you

Try to empty all the air in your gut

Take your time

The longer your exhale is, the calmer you'll feel

Now, start inhaling through your nose slowly

Very slowly

Just try to feel everything about this air

Feel the sensation this air creates in your nostrils

Does it feel cool or warm?

Can you feel any kind of fragrance?

As you inhale

Follow the path of the air through your awareness

Store as much air as you can

The more fresh air you breathe

The more relaxed you'll feel

Just don't stress yourself

Let things be easy

When you're ready

Exhale through your mouth

Role your lips a bit so that the air makes a hissing sound as it exits your mouth

This is the sound of relaxation

Keep emptying all the air that's inside you

Let everything come out

Feel your belly going towards your back as you push out the air

Let the calm prevail over you

Once you've exhaled fully relax

Just feel the relaxation

Observe the stress levels going down

When you are ready, start inhaling again

Breathe in through your nose to the count of 5

1....

2....

3......

4.......

5.........

Hold this air briefly

Only for a few moments

Now exhale through your mouth to the count of 7

1....

2....

3......

4.......

5.........

6.........

7..........

Relax!

Repeat the process a few more times

Breathe in through your nose to the count of 5

1....

2....

3......

4.......

5.........

Hold this air briefly

Only for a few moments

Now exhale through your mouth to the count of 7

1....

2....

3......

4.......

5.........

6.........

7..........

Relax!

One more time,

Breathe in through your nose to the count of 5

1....

2....

3......

4.......

5.........

Hold this air briefly

Only for a few moments

Now exhale through your mouth to the count of 7

1....

2....

3......

4.......

5.........

6.........

7..........

Relax!

Now once again observe your breathing

Is it rhythmic now?

As you practice deep breathing, your breathing rate becomes slow

It induces calm, and you start feeling more relaxed.

You can repeat the process as many times as you want

When you start feeling calm, you can open your eyes

Again, do not show any haste

Let your body find its pace.

Meditation

Meditation is the oldest method of unifying the mind, body, and spirit. The oldest mention of meditation is found in Indus valley civilization paintings. Vedas, the sacred Hindu texts, have an elaborate mention of meditation and the impact it can have on our lives and understanding. Vedas describe meditation as the way to completely get connected to the mind. It is the ultimate way to get out of the trap. This lays and broadens our understanding.

Even Buddhists consider meditation as the ultimate way to achieve liberation. They believe that if you want to get out of the vicious cycle of pain and pleasure, then meditation is the correct way. It evolved by various names, but the purpose is the same in all.

There are several misconceptions about meditation. People have associated with difficult positions and complicated the whole thing. You don't need to worry about any of that.

Meditation is the best way to put your stress aside and focus on broader issues. It helps you in building a better perspective. It is a technique that also helps you in adopting a fearless and positive attitude. When you meditate, you realize that there is nothing that you need to fear as everything is inside you, and you are that everything.

You can use positive affirmations while you meditate to propagate positivity. You can use it to untangle your thoughts. You can also use it to face your fears head-on.

We will now do a short meditation session. You can also record the given meditation in your own voice to use it as a guided meditation.

There is no specific time to practice relaxation meditation. You can practice this meditation anytime you feel stressed.

You would need half an hour of uninterrupted time.

Simply get seated in a comfortable position.

If possible, you can sit in a cross-legged position, or you can also do it while sitting on a chair

Your clothing should be comfortable. It shouldn't be restrictive. If you are in your formals, simply loosen them a little.

Sit with your back upright. This is important.

Either you meditate in a seated position or while lying down, your spine should be straight.

If you want, you can use a backrest to keep your spine straight

Keep your neck straight

Your neck shouldn't be bending forward or sideways

You should never use a neck rest

Now keep your hands in your lap on top of each other and relax!

Guided Meditation

With your back and neck straight try to relax

Don't try to think anything specific

There is no need to force your mind

If you are comfortable, you can close your eyes gently

If you feel more anxious with your eyes closed, simply fix your gaze at one point in front of your eyes

It can be anything; you can also put any object for better focus

Now relax!

Simply breathe in

And

Breathe out

Breathe in

Breathe out

Breathe in

Breathe out

Breathe in

Breathe out

Now bring your awareness to your breathing

Just focus on the way you are breathing

Are you breathing fast?

Is it slow?

Are you able to breathe rhythmically?

Don't judge the way you are breathing

Simply observe it

Breathing is a majestic process

We never pay attention to it

Pay attention to the way you are inhaling

The way each breath goes in

Travels through your whole respiratory system and then comes out

Nothing is hidden

The process is clear

Yet we never pay attention to it

Breathe in

Breathe out

Breathe in

Breathe out

Breathe in

Breathe out

Breathe in

Breathe out

Breathe in

Breathe out

There is no need to control anything

Let everything flow naturally

Let the life energy come in through your nostrils

Let this fresh air calm all the anxiety inside you

Breathe in

Breathe out

Breathe in

Breathe out

Breathe in

Breathe out

Again observe your breathing

Is it still rapid?

Has it regained its natural pace?

If you are still breathing rapidly

Simply keep breathing with focus

Breathe in

Breathe out

Breathe in

Breathe out

Breathe in

Breathe out

Now we will do deep breathing

Breathe in through your nose to the count of 5

1....

2....

3......

4.......

5.........

Hold this air briefly

Only for a few moments

Now exhale through your mouth to the count of 7

1....

2....

3......

4.......

5.........

6.........

7..........

Relax!

Repeat the process a few more times

Breathe in through your nose to the count of 5

1....

2....

3......

4.......

5.........

Hold this air briefly

Only for a few moments

Now exhale through your mouth to the count of 7

1....

2....

3......

4.......

5.........

6.........

7..........

Relax!

Breathe in through your nose to the count of 5

1....

2....

3......

4.......

5.........

Hold this air briefly

Only for a few moments

Now exhale through your mouth to the count of 7

1....

2....

3......

4.......

5.........

6.........

7..........

Relax!

Observe your breathing once again

Is it calm?

Are you feeling calmer?

Are you still feeling anxious?

Now shift your awareness to your head

You are just going to be an observer

Simply look at the thoughts you are having

Don't judge the thoughts

Don't label your thoughts as positive or negative

Simply look at them

Observe the way thoughts originate in your mind

Try to identify any thought flowing in your mind

Can you pick one?

You don't need to indulge

Simply follow the thought

Observe the speed with which the mind processes several thoughts at the same time

See how quickly thoughts take shape

How they can completely change

Now pick another one

All the thoughts are a creation of your mind

They have no real presence

You have the power to change their course

You also have the power to think selectively

Your mind is a part of you

Bring your awareness back to your breathing

Observe your breathing

Is it deep?

Are you feeling relaxed?

You can practice deep breathing for as long as you want

Open your eyes gently when you are ready.

Relax

Don't try to get up immediately

Give your body some time to react

You can get up whenever you want

Visualization

Visualization is also a meditation technique, but it is done using guided imageries. You can use any kind of soothing imagery like a walk in the park, a trek to a forest, a picknick near a river, or anything else that calms your mind.

Because you use soothing imageries, it is very easy to divert the mind from the current issue that's causing the stress, and hence, it helps in bringing relaxation faster. You are able to calm easily, and even getting out of very serious bouts of anger becomes easy.

There is no limit to the kind of imageries you can use. In fact, you can also use imageries that might invoke your past traumatic experiences. This might sound painful, but it helps a lot in making them less fearful. As you do this, consciously facing them becomes easier. Soon their fear goes away, and you are able to free yourself from the clutch of those experiences.

Therefore, the use of visualizations is wide. As you get comfortable with the process, you can experiment and find your comfort level.

Here we will use one simple guided imagery of a beautiful park to invoke positivity.

Sit with your back upright. This is important.

Either you meditate in a seated position or while lying down, your spine should be straight.

If you want, you can use a backrest to keep your spine straight

Keep your neck straight

Your neck shouldn't be bending forward or sideways

You should never use a neck rest

Now keep your hands in your lap on top of each other and relax!

With your back and neck straight try to relax

Don't try to think anything specific

There is no need to force your mind

If you are comfortable, you can close your eyes gently

If you feel more anxious with your eyes closed, simply fix your gaze at one point in front of your eyes

It can be anything; you can also put any object for better focus

Now relax!

Simply breathe in

And

Breathe out

Breathe in

Breathe out

Breathe in

Breathe out

Breathe in

Breathe out

Now bring your awareness to your breathing

Just focus on the way you are breathing

Are you breathing fast?

Is it slow?

Are you able to breathe rhythmically?

Don't judge the way you are breathing

Simply observe it

Breathing is a majestic process

We never pay attention to it

Pay attention to the way you are inhaling

The way each breath goes in

Travels through your whole respiratory system and then comes out

Nothing is hidden

The process is clear

Yet we never pay attention to it

Breathe in

Breathe out

Breathe in

Breathe out

Breathe in

Breathe out

Breathe in

Breathe out

Breathe in

Breathe out

There is no need to control anything

Let everything flow naturally

Let the life energy come in through your nostrils

Let this fresh air calm all the anxiety inside you

Breathe in

Breathe out

Breathe in

Breathe out

Breathe in

Breathe out

Again observe your breathing

Is it still rapid?

Has it regained its natural pace?

If you are still breathing rapidly

Simply keep breathing with focus

Breathe in

Breathe out

Breathe in

Breathe out

Breathe in

Breathe out

Now we will do deep breathing

Breathe in through your nose to the count of 5

1....

2....

3......

4.......

5.........

Hold this air briefly

Only for a few moments

Now exhale through your mouth to the count of 7

1....

2....

3……

4…….

5………

6………

7……….

Relax!

Repeat the process a few more times

Breathe in through your nose to the count of 5

1….

2….

3……

4…….

5………

Hold this air briefly

Only for a few moments

Now exhale through your mouth to the count of 7

1….

2….

3……

4…….

5………

6………

7……….

Relax!

Breathe in through your nose to the count of 5

1….

2….

3……

4…….

5………

Hold this air briefly

Only for a few moments

Now exhale through your mouth to the count of 7

1….

2….

3……

4.......

5.........

6.........

7..........

Relax!

Observe your breathing once again

Is it calm?

Are you feeling calmer?

Are you still feeling anxious?

Now shift your awareness to the center of your forehead

Try to find a point of light somewhere at the center

Visualize the spinning vortex of light expanding slowly

It is growing rapidly and covering everything around it

It is making you feel giddy

You seem to be losing focus

The vortex has become larger than you

It is in front of you as a portal to a new world

You want to explore it

You are apprehensive

There is no need to worry

It is only your awareness

There is no danger

No harm can come to you

Step inside it

On the other side, you are still very cautious

But you find your feet on solid footing

This place looks different

You can't really place the location

It seems to be some garden

In fact, a very beautiful one

You can smell the fragrance of several flowers

There is also the smell of ripe fruits

This is even stranger

It is not the season

Under your feet, you can also feel the cushion of the grass

This encourages you to move ahead

So much pleasantness can't lead you into a trap

It is a beautiful garden

There are huge trees laden with fruits and flowers

Exotic fruits of all kinds

The grass below is laden with flowers

There are trees on both sides of the pathway

It is a well-maintained garden

The branches are providing adequate shade

You don't know where this path leads, but you are now feeling encouraged and intrigued to find

Look on the right; there was some movement

It felt as if some animal was there

Oh! It's a beautiful deer

It's looking so stunning

It isn't even looking towards you

It isn't afraid of you
It seems here no one can cause any harm
On the left, there are so beautiful flowers
Rows of flowers
White, violet, orange, pink
It is a strange color combination
But, it is soothing to the eyes
Nothing flashy
Simply soothing

Down the road you see some kids playing
They've seen you coming
They don't look alarmed or concerned
There is a sense of calm in the air
A feeling of safety and carelessness
No one seems to be bothered by your presence

There is a small pond in front
The water is looking crystal clear

You can see multicolored fishes swimming in it

You sit down beside the pool

It is time to relax

There has been so much haste

There is no more the need for haste

You don't even feel the energy for it

You want to cool down

There has been a lot of senselessness

Sitting beside the pool will help in gaining some sense back

It will give you the time to think

So much has been going on

Are you feeling happy about these things?

Do you want life to go at the same pace?

Are you happy with its direction?

Are you really doing anything specific?

Life is not about repentance

It is about changing the destiny

It is about taking the right steps

It is not the time to fall back

You have the power to bring the change

You can't blame others for everything

You feel so much stressed

The journey has also induced this fatigue

Get the weight off your shoulders

It's a backpack

Look at it

There's nothing useful in it

You are simply carrying things on your shoulders that cause stress

It is time you got rid of them

No need to carry them

Simply dispose of it

You see a dumpster in front of you

It is the right place to get rid of this bag

Just dump it there as it is

Don't even carry the empty bag with you

When there is a bag, you tend to fill it with the useless burden

Get rid of everything

Start with a clean slate

Let it be a new beginning

You are feeling extremely light now

The bag wasn't very heavy

But the feeling of getting rid of it is much better

Now, sit back and relax

Think of all the good things that have happened recently

All the pleasurable moments that you've experienced

All the stress has dissipated

You are feeling completely refreshed

It is getting darker

You have spent a lot of time here

It is time to return now

You have enjoyed the experience

You can return anytime you want

Let's get back

You once again look at the things you saw while coming

Everything is as it was

Everything is reassuring that the experience was real

You are walking back leisurely

There is no hurry

You have reached the portal

You once again look back

You want to fill your eyes with the experience

As you cross the portal, you watch the vortex getting smaller

Within seconds it has again become a dot

Bring your awareness back to your breathing

Is your breathing rhythmic?

Are you breathing deeply?

Are you feeling completely relaxed?

Simply observe your breathing

Inhale

Exhale

Inhale

Exhale

Inhale

Exhale

Try to feel your surrounding through your awareness

Any noise that you can hear

You can open your eyes whenever you want.

Relax!

Mindfulness

Mindfulness is another technique to remove stress from our lives. It is one of the most widely appreciated ways to live a relaxed life.

Mindfulness is nothing but a phenomenon of becoming more aware of everything you do, feel, or think. It means that when you start doing things mindfully, you fully understand them and feel them to the core. Even a simple act of walking doesn't remain only the movement of limbs, but you start feeling every movement and find a purpose in it.

You just don't pick anything and start eating. It is a process you respect completely and pay attention to the food. A mindful person would feel every morsel of food in the mouth and wouldn't simply wash things down the throat.

There is a purpose behind such close attention. A major reason for the stress in our lives is our mindlessness. We have started living in our minds. We assume everything and feel nothing. The fashion of multitasking has taken the love of doing anything at all. This means we are literally living a mindless life. Most of our actions don't have real meaning, even to us. We eat several times a day without understanding the purpose that food solves. We run without the benefit it gives. We do our jobs without ever thinking about its merits. The jobs we do don't have any real meaning for us, and neither we mean anything to that job.

Everything around us, including us, has become meaningless. Mindfulness is a way to put some sense into all this.

You learn to do everything carefully. From the simple tasks like eating to the job you do, it is a process of paying due attention to everything.

These days one of the reasons for such high stress is our mindlessness. We have stopped paying attention to things, and hence, our mind has a lot of free time to things all the things it wants. Mindfulness breaks it.

Close observation becomes a part of your life, and this brings down stress in life significantly.

You can opt for mindfulness for a stress-free life. It is a simple and effective technique to lower the useless stress that we wear as a cloak.

Hypnosis

Hypnosis is another way to relax the mind quickly. If you are feeling highly stressed and want to calm down fast, you can also take the help of hypnosis.

Hypnosis is an intriguing subject. It is a power we all want to gain. Have you wondered about the ease of work if you could hypnotize people around you or hold them by your charm? That may be difficult, but hypnosis can surely help you in cooling down.

Hypnotherapy is used even by some psychiatrists to look into the depth of the patient's mind. It opens those doors in the mind that are usually kept tightly shut.

Due to this power, hypnotherapy has the potential to provide relaxation. It is a tool through which you inspire your mind to relax. The mind starts to relax easily, and then passing into a deep sleep is comparatively easy.

Therefore, if a person is suffering from high stress and is unable to sleep at all or wants to relax, hypnosis can help to a great extent.

Sleep hypnosis can also be induced by playing music at certain wavelengths. You can also download hypnosis videos from the internet and use them for sleeping.

It is important to understand that hypnosis doesn't work in the same manner for everyone. Some people find it very easy to relax, listening to sleep hypnosis while others don't get similar results. Therefore, you may have to try it to find its effectiveness for you.

Laughing Out Loud

Laughing out loud is an amazing way to bring down your stress. Nothing affects your body and mind more effectively than laughter.

When you laugh, a number of chemical and physiological reactions begin.

- As you laugh your body starts releasing endorphins also known as happy hormones
- Laughter has a very relaxing effect, and there is a physiological process behind it. When you laugh your blood pressure, and heart rate goes up for a short while, and that induces the feeling of relaxation
- It also improves the air and blood circulation in the body bringing a soothing effect
- It stimulates most of your vital organs like your heart, lungs, brain, and muscles
- Laughter is also a natural pain reliever
- It improves your immune system, mood, and behavior

You may think that if you are already laughing, then there wouldn't be any stress in the first place. Why do you need the advice then?

Laughing is a process, and even imitating the process while you are not finding anything particularly funny will have a similar effect. This means that if you are feeling highly stressed and fear an anxiety attack, you can prevent it if you start laughing loudly. This is called laughter therapy. You'd be surprised to know that it is also used in helping patients suffering from cancer.

It is an easy, effective, and pocket-friendly option to get rid of stress.

Stress Diet

Our body plays a very important role in the amount of stress we carry. The stress has a deep physiological impact, and hence, looking at it simply in emotional or mental terms would be an injustice. If anything has a physiological impact, then the kind of food we eat would have a role to play in it.

The kind of food we eat can matter a lot in our day to day stress. Some foods will have a naturally calming effect, and they will lower the production of stress hormones. It is easy to guess that such foods will have a positive impact on the level of stress in your body.

There are certain food items that are inflammatory in nature, and they can create serious stress. Consumption of alcohol, tobacco, and coffee can also have a similar impact.

In fact, there are certain food items that look harmless but can simply agitate your system and lead to stress.

It is important to understand the things that can be consumed safely and would lower the stress on the body.

Simple Carbs: Stress is high energy-consuming, and while your body is in stress, it needs a lot of glucose. In the case of chronic stress, you may always feel energy starved. In such a condition, foods that provide instant energy are relaxing to the body. Simple carbs like sweets, chocolates, refined flour items are easy to process, and hence, your body loves them. These foods lead to the release of serotonin, also known as the comfort hormone. So, if you are feeling stressed, you can have these things, but the consumption should always be kept a bare minimum. These foods can become addictive.

Complex carbs: Complex carbs are the best for your body. The digestive system takes a very long time to process these carbs, and they also provide a lot of fiber to your system, which is very good for your gut. Complex carbs also contain a lot of trace minerals required by your body, and hence, consuming them is good for your body. When the quantity of complex carbs is balanced, your body finds it easy to recover from stress.

Oranges: Stress puts a lot of pressure on the immune system. Under stress, the cortisol levels go up as well as the blood pressure also shoots up. Vitamin C intake can boost your immunity in such a case. Oranges are naturally rich in vitamin C, and you must consume them in good quantities. An important thing to note is that you must try to eat the orange fruit in place of orange juice. The pulp is as important as the juice. If you still want to drink it, then make a shake or smoothie, but don't simply rely on juice that comes without pulp.

Nuts: Stress has a very poor impact on your cholesterol and, ultimately, your heart. We have been fed that cholesterol is bad for our heart. So all our effort is directed towards reducing the cholesterol intake. This is simply half-truth. The cholesterol is as important for our body, as is our blood. It is the building block for many hormones and works as the repair material for all the damage that occurs to our heart. Cholesterol is not the problem but the damage that our heart bears due to stress, chronic inflammation, ischemic injuries inflicted by a sudden shock. When the heart vessels get injured, the cholesterol simply sticks to the walls to prevent blood seepage. If the injuries are frequent, the repair will keep getting thicker. If you want to save your heart, then you will have to work towards lowering stress, that is the main cause of injuries. Eating food items that help in lowering some bad cholesterol and VLDL is important. Nuts, fibrous foods, and anti-inflammatory foods can play a very important role in it.

Fatty Fish- Fatty fish is very good for your health as it is rich in Omega-3 fatty acids, which help in reducing inflammation. You must consume good quality fatty fish regularly for getting an adequate amount of omega-3 fatty acids.

Leafy Greens- Leafy greens are another major source of antioxidants. They also provide a lot of minerals that your body needs, and hence, they also help your body in dealing with stress. You must consume 7-10 cups of leafy greens daily to get the required amount of antioxidants, flavonoids, vitamins, and minerals.

Raw Vegetables- Raw vegetables are again very good for your body as they have a lot of vitamins, minerals, and antioxidants. In addition to that, they also provide a lot of digestible fiber required by the body. They keep your gut health and immune system working. You must consume a lot of raw vegetables in stressful conditions.

Black tea and green tea: To counter stress better, it is essential to get rid of coffee. In place of it, you can drink black tea, and green tea as these beverages help in lowering inflammation and make you feel calmer.

Vitamins and Minerals: Vitamin B2, B6, and C are very important to counter stress, and you must consume them in good proportions. If you feel that your diet lacks these vitamins, you can also take them as supplements after consulting the dose with your doctors. Along with these minerals like magnesium and calcium are also important.

Goal Setting

Stress reduction is a tough but workable goal. However, if you think you'll be able to achieve it without proper planning and management, then you are going to get disappointed.

Stress is not like other problems. It is the Problem. Stress is life can throw your life in a frenzy. The first thing you lose during stress is control. It is the loss of control that primarily leads to stress. Hence, if you are really serious about reducing stress in your life, setting goals is very important.

When you are under chronic stress, it is very easy to get off track. Prioritizing is a fairly difficult task for people suffering from chronic stress. It is unlike any other problem. The first thing that it affects is your power to reason logically. You take most decisions either impulsively or aggressively. The touch of calm is missing in it.

To get out of the vicious cycle of stress, it is important to

1. Set the right achievable goals
2. Make actionable plans to achieve those goals
3. Follow those plans

However, if you look closely, for most people, the very goals can become a reason for stress. At the first sign of failure to achieve a milestone, the first instinct would be to drop the whole plan, and this is a universal attitude for people under stress. They start thinking about making another more actionable plan that would never come up.

Goal setting for stress management is a very important task. It is a task you must do very carefully. You must keep in mind all the important variables. Keeping the stressors in mind and well as your reactions to them is very important while you set your goals.

The most important thing that you need to keep in mind while setting your goals is to keep your daily stressors to the lowest.

Your goals must help you in dealing with stressors in two crucial areas.

1. Stressors at the workplace
2. Stressors at home

How to Set Goals?

In the beginning, your focus should be to minimize and manage stress.

You should have five major goals in mind:

1. Work on Stressors
2. Employ Stress Management Techniques
3. Develop Stress Relieving Habits
4. Develop Emotional Resilience
5. Try to Find Avenues of Happiness

The goals have been sequenced as per priority, but you can work on all of them together if you can. Simply remember that while you work on the fifth, you can't ignore the first. No major change would come until you meet the first three goals.

Work on Stressors

Identify and Remove Major Stressors

Writing this book, it is impossible for me to guess the things that can stress you the most. But, whatever they are must be identified and removed. This is a top priority task. If you are thinking of moving ahead without accomplishing this task, you are not likely to succeed.

Here, it is important to understand that we are talking about changeable stressors. If deadlines stress you the most, then, does it mean that you would completely stop working and leave your job? That's an impractical solution.

If deadlines cause the highest amount of stress, then start taking less work. Don't let the pressure build whenever a task is assigned to start working from the very instant. Don't wait for the next day to start. It must be your target to finish the task much ahead of the task.

Whatever the stressor is, you will have to ensure that you identify it clearly and get rid of it. Stress management is not about working with stress. There is no way one can work with stress. You simply need to work around it.

Practice Meditation Regularly to Face Stressors Calmly

Meditation is one of the most reliable ways to counter all kinds of stressors. Meditation helps you in broadening your perspective. It gives you a positive outlook, and hence, you are able to remain neutral even in negative situations. This isn't a fight to get victory over stressors. We are simply trying to dodge or remain undefeated.

Your most sincere attempt should be to avoid stressors as far as possible, but life as we know it always works in an unpredictable manner. This means that there can be times when you come face to face with the stressors. In those circumstances, you must not lose your calm and composer, and this is what meditation helps you with.

- It gives you a broader perspective
- It lowers your reactivity to stress
- It makes you very calm and resilient

Adopt an Optimistic Attitude

Stressors affect us the most because,in the first instance of stress, our threat perception starts running lose. It is a negative attitude that we have towards life. One way to deal with this attitude is to develop a positive attitude.

Become optimistic in life. Optimism is an approach, and it takes time to make it a part of your life. You simply can't choose to become optimistic in the face of the problem. Therefore, now is the best time to start.

Optimism gives you great confidence that will be helpful in several ways to fight stress in life.

Exercise Daily

Physical exercise also makes you better equipped to deal with mental and emotional stress. Any kind of stress is ultimately going to affect your body. If you hear a piece of bad news, your heart will start pumping fast; your blood pressure would increase, the release of stress hormones would take place. All these are physical reactions, and hence, you can't say that any stress is purely mental or emotional.

Now, suppose you are physically fit and have been exercising regularly. The impact of stress on your body would be less. This also means that your reaction may not be extreme. Remember that stress is simply your body's reaction. The greater the effect, the stronger the reaction. It is a simple third law of motion. If your body is absorbing the shock better, it won't react that aggressively.

Make exercise a part of your daily routine.

Employ Stress Relief Techniques

There are several techniques that can be employed to lower stress in daily life. We will discuss all these techniques in detail in the next part. Here, we'll simply stick to basic explanation and use.

Deep Breathing

Deep breathing is a very powerful technique to lower stress. You can employ this technique anywhere. It would help you in battling current stress very effectively.

Meditation

As we have already discussed, meditation is a great way to lower stress in day to day life. You must do meditation at least once a day and, if possible, twice.

Body Scan Meditation

This is also a type of meditation that can help you in relaxing your body and mind. This meditation technique uses breathing with your awareness to relax individual muscles in the body, and the effect is amazing. It can help in lowering physical and mental stress significantly.

Loving Kindness Meditation

This meditation is very helpful in developing a forgiving and grateful attitude towards others. If you practice this meditation every morning as you get up, you'll experience a tremendous change in your attitude. You'll find yourself feeling less angry and anxious.

Laughter Therapy

This is again a process of simply laughing out loud as often as possible and especially when you are feeling stressed and frustrated. The laugh would be forced and but the impact would be genuine.

Visualization

Visualization is a meditation technique that helps in calming the mind and lowering stress by imagining various scenarios. This meditation also has a very positive impact on lowering stress.

Mindfulness

Mindfulness is the practice of becoming aware of everything that you do. A mindful person starts making conscious decisions about every aspect of life and takes every action consciously. Living in the present is the quality of this style of living.

Develop Stress Relieving Habits

Ask for Hug from Loved Ones

Love has stress canceling power. When feeling stress, ask your loved ones to give you a tight hug. The personal touch has a very healing quality. When someone who loves you gives you a hug, your body releases a hormone called oxytocin; this has a very positive effect on your mood.

Aromatherapy

It has been found that certain scents can trigger positive areas in the brain. Taking aromatherapy regularly can keep these areas triggered, and hence, you will be able to counter stress in a much better way.

Creative Hobbies

Creative hobbies give your mind a positive engagement. This also means that your mind gets less time to ponder over useless things, and hence, you will be able to cope with stress better.

Eat a Balanced Diet

Eating a balanced diet can also have a very positive impact on your stress levels. A positive diet keeps your stress level low, and hence, you are easily able to remain happy.

Everyday Take out Time for Leisure Activities

You should take out time for some kind of joyful physical activity daily. From gardening to swimming, you can choose whatever you feel like, but there should be something that keeps you pleasantly occupied for some time every day. It should be an activity you look up to. This will instill positivity, and there would be things you would eagerly wait for. Not only this, in case of any stress in the day, you would get an avenue to positively take out all the stress.

Do Positive Self-Talk

Positive affirmations are great as they keep you inspired, but positive self-talk is even better. Most of us can do self-criticism. It comes naturally. However, positive self-talk is something you need to cultivate. But it has a great impact on your personality. Once we start acknowledging our own abilities and qualities, our confidence increases several times over.

Express Gratitude More Often

Our failure to acknowledge the efforts of others is also a major cause of concern. We simply keep trying to find fault in others and don't really appreciate their efforts. This creates another problem, and that's discontent. We become difficult to please, and as much it is a problem for others, it is also a problem for us. Unknowingly we develop a grumpy attitude, which leads to stress.

We keep feeling resentment against others even for obsolete things, and it all keeps adding up. Expressing gratitude more often in public can get us out of this trap. It can also fill us with more positivity as we would feel happy about others and wouldn't have reason to be angry.

Maintain To-Do List Religiously

Maintaining a To-Do list is very important. If you want to keep stress at bay, you must make a to-do list daily and keep updating it. This will prevent you from missing out on important things and the resultant stress.

Develop Emotional Resilience

Stress has the greatest impact on our emotions. However, some people can start feeling overwhelmed, while others may not show any significant reaction. It all depends on an individual's ability to handle stress.

Some individuals may be able to process even negative events calmly, while others may not be able to show the same resilience. It all varies from person to person. However, even if you don't have that gift, it can be developed. You can also become resilient to stress.

Following things can help you in developing resilience:

Emotional Awareness

Most people are unable to clearly define their emotional reactions. They can start showing different reactions to similar events. It is just the need to have a reaction to an adverse event that works. It is important to develop emotional awareness. Identify your triggers and then start assessing your reactions. Soon you'll observe that you have better control over your emotions.

Get Over Victim Mentality

Most people are never really come out of victim mentality, and that's why they start showing earth-shattering reactions. If you want to develop better emotional resilience, you must get over the victim mentality. Your reactions must be according to the situation.

Social Support

People with stronger social support tend to be emotionally resilient as they find people behind them in terms of adverse conditions. This makes them fearless. People with poor social support won't be able to find this confidence and may show an exaggerated reaction.

Good Sense of Humor

Develop a good sense of humor. It is essential and helpful for yourself and others. A person with a good sense of humor will be able to laugh off a difficulty much better.

Spirituality

Spiritual inclination can also play a very important role to have stronger emotional resilience. The people who have spiritual inclination find a stronger force to lean on. They generally don't feel lonely in times of trouble, and hence, their reactions are more contained.

Redefine Happiness

Most of us are bound by the social conventions of happiness. A person with a stable career, big house, big car, good bank balance, and a family must be a happy person. This is a general idea. People forget that happiness is subjective. Every person can have an entirely different definition of happiness. However, most of us never get a chance to define happiness for ourselves. We simply get trained to look at things and believe they would give happiness. If I don't enjoy watching TV, even a 300-inch TV would have no meaning for me. A homosexual man would find no pleasure in marrying the most beautiful women in the world. It is important that you define your own happiness and start building your world around it.

Conclusion

Thank you for making it through to the end of this book, let's hope it was informative and able to provide you with all of the tools you need to achieve your goals whatever they may be.

Stress is a real issue, and it affects all of us on some level. The problem is that most of us are never able to identify its real extent before it is too late.

Even simple behavioral changes can reflect stress in life, but most of us remain ignorant about them.

Stress not only affects us emotionally and behaviorally, but it also has a deep and severe physiological impact on which most people remain completely unaware.

Not knowing something doesn't mean it would affect us any less.

If stress is not encountered at the right time, getting over it can be very difficult. Many people keep struggling all their lives but are never fully able to recover.

Most people completely surrender to unchangeable stressors and are forced to spend miserable lives, although they had a real chance to recover.

This book has tried to cover all that so that you don't remain affected due to ignorance and get a real chance to overcome stress in life.

This book has laid out plans, tips and tricks, and practical techniques through which you can overcome stress.

I hope that you will be able to make use of this information in a practical and meaningful way.

Every effort has been made to ensure the accuracy of the facts.

I hope that you will be able to reap the benefits of mindfulness in your personal life, and this book would be useful in the process.

Finally, if you found this book useful in any way, a review on Amazon is always appreciated!

Description

Do you want to overcome stress at work and home from the first day without spending a dime in therapy, counseling, and consultation?

Stress is a menace that affects everyone. Do you think you'll be less affected by it if you didn't know it?

This is a misconception that most people have. They believe that only the people who have to see a doctor are suffering from stress.

Stress affects all of us because it is our body's natural reaction. The problem begins when this reaction is serious and becomes chronic.

More than 110 million Americans are currently affected by prediabetes or diabetes, but most are ignorant about it.

Does that make them less susceptible to danger?

The same is the case with stress. The overall stress level of American society is much above the acceptable level, and that even includes kids. In reality, a much greater population is currently battling with high stress which is affecting them emotionally, behaviorally, and physiologically.

Did you know that stress can have a deep impact on your physical health too?

Most people have a very vague knowledge of stress, and they would clearly fail to identify clear signals of stress. This means they might be overlooking their own real health issues as well as the issues faced by their loved ones.

This book will help you in understanding:

- The real depth and penetration of stress
- Types of stress and how it matters to us
- Impact of stress on our body, mental, and emotional health as well as behavior
- The real terms in which you need to identify stressors
- Ways in which you can bring down stress at the workplace
- Ways in which you can bring down stress in your personal life
- Ways in which you can deal with your mind causing the stress
- More importantly, ways to deal with unchangeable stressors
- Techniques like meditation, visualization, mindfulness, and goal setting that can help in bring down stress

And much more....

CPSIA information can be obtained
at www.ICGtesting.com
Printed in the USA
BVHW041554261020
591851BV00004B/22

9 781801 123211